BLESSED
ARE THE WEIRD
A MANIFESTO FOR CREATIVES

BLESSED
ARE THE WEIRD
A MANIFESTO FOR CREATIVES

JACOB NORDBY

Published in the United States of America
Manifesto Publishing House, Inc. 2016
Boise, ID 83703
www.manifestopublishing.com

emtippettsbookdesigns.com

For Nathan

"Without deviation from the norm, progress is not possible."
– Frank Zappa

"The big question is whether you are going to be able to say a hearty yes to your adventure."
- Joseph Campbell

INTRODUCTION

Ancient texts and recent discoveries suggest that human civilization had once advanced to levels nearly as high as our own—maybe every bit as high. The records are spotty, but information patterns are emerging to reveal that we have likely "been here before."

Then, it would appear, something happened. It seems possible that an extremely advanced worldwide civilization came crashing down in an apocalypse so thorough and widespread that it nearly erased all memory of what had been.

Nearly.

Fragments of those memories are resurfacing now as we approach another zenith in human progress. As the puzzle pieces show up in mysterious and timely ways, we are forced to ask questions about who we are, what we are doing, and if maybe … just maybe … this time could be different.

Among these hints and shadows of what might have come before, one warning stands out—when humans create a world that is wildly out of sync with the laws of nature, disaster strikes as an inevitable rebalancing occurs.

We have created such a world and we have done so with blinding speed and momentum. It is almost as if the ant pile got kicked over tens of thousands of years ago, leaving just a few behind to rebuild things in the wake of some disaster. But, like ants do, we did rebuild, and the world that we have created seems to be reaching the tipping point once again.

The world's religions and ancient wisdom traditions have various stories about what might have happened "back then"—great floods, a giant meteorite strike, a human-created technological disaster that may have involved worldwide conflict that ended in a nuclear-style bang, or some invasion from external cosmic forces.

The specifics are not clear and I am not willing to speculate about any particular story. In fact, as Joseph Campbell once said, "Literalism is idolatry." To get wound up in details and chase around trying to prove or disprove everything would merely block us from seeing a pattern of information that is emerging and begs for our attention.

This information suggests that when humans unconsciously create, create, create out of fight-or-flight reaction to the forces of nature (and each other) in an effort to secure our own safety, we ultimately develop a lopsided, out-of-balance situation that is doomed to implode.

Part of the challenge with this line of thinking is that if you look back over the course of progress for all of history as we know it, the way we have done it makes sense. We used our rational, process-and-judgment oriented minds to solve the problems of survival on this harsh little planet. To a large degree, we invented our way out of hardship and out of a position of being victims to the caprice of nature. We have running water; predictable food supplies; solid houses that protect us from the wind, rain, snow, and sun; air conditioning; and all manner of machines that are supposed to make our lives much easier. Most of us don't live in caves. From that perspective, what we have built is practical and logical. It makes sense.

But there is a deep sense of anxiety that pervades our entire civilizaton right now. Something is not right. All of our machines and finely-tuned processes and the massive acceleration of life's pace are starting to sound and feel a lot like a poorly loaded washing machine that goes "whomp ... whomp ... whomp ... whomp-whomp-WHOMP-WHOMP-WHOMMMMP!" when the spin cycle takes off.

Something doesn't feel right. Something is telling us that there is imbalance in the world, perhaps as a result of all of our advances. The "something" doesn't make sense, which is why we have a hard time paying attention to it. We have idolized the scientific method and the rational process to such a degree that anything trying to speak to us from the irrational or the symbolic is easy to ignore. It also makes us uneasy with its persistent way of appearing at the edges of our awareness like shadow presences that flit in the corners of our eyes but disappear as soon as we look directly at them.

This something is what might be called Soul—the vast aspect of us that dwells outside the boundaries of reason and communicates using strange symbols, intuitive nudges, impulses of desire, dreams, and unnamable (but insatiable) longings. It speaks in stories and music and paintings and sculptures. It hides messages in songs and clues in poetry. It runs down our cheeks in tears when something deeply true is said. It steps invisibly into plain sight when we walk into wild places where our cell phones don't work.

We inhabit a clanking, rusty machine world that we have all built together down through the course of these many, many generations. It has a shiny modern exterior, but the insides are dry as a desert and we are exhausted by the demand to keep it all running no matter what.

We, the world, want our soul back. We are parched for it. We are starving for it. We are also afraid that to pursue it means giving up everything we have built along the way.

We believe that this is a sucker's choice—either-or.

But there is an "and" option—a third way. In our binary-dominated world, it is all too easy to notice just on/off, black/white, yes/no. We need more options. We are being asked by the times in which we live to find a middle road—some way to navigate out of the tired old ruts.

This middle road is often crooked and narrow. Carlos Castaneda called it "the path with heart." Joseph Campbell taught us to find it when he said, "Follow your bliss." One of Carl Jung's clients, troubled by the looming state of things, asked him, "Dr. Jung, can the world escape an apocalypse?" Jung replied, "If enough people do their inner work." He was describing the great journey of individual soul excavation—and this book is meant to be a signpost along the road of that adventure.

A group of people has traveled this path since before time as we know it began. I call them the Blessed Weird people. They have been the keepers of offbeat wisdom throughout history. I say offbeat because what they have been doing has rarely followed the normal trajectory of progress.

Before the machine age took hold, these creative "weird people" held a special place and were cared for by wealthy patrons because what they did was considered essential to human well-being. They were part of the *avant-garde*, leading the forward edge of progress with their paintings, poems, sculptures, symphonies, and inventions. Not all of them were the sequestered beneficiaries of the powerful, though. Looking back, there was a time when many artists were not widely separated from those who created practical things. They were often the same people.

Artisans once crafted every utilitarian implement of life—the saddles and dishes and saltboxes and forks and armor and blankets and everything else. That was before we invented ways to produce the goods we need in factories. Art was intertwined with life. Artisans and craftspeople burned, stamped, or carved brands and trademarks into what they had made with their own hands as marks of pride in their work. The things they produced to be used in everyday life meant something both to those who made them and those who purchased them in ways that can't be easily understood by modern consumers who fill our houses and garages and storage units with stuff made by people in some faraway place and to whom we have no connection.

My youngest brother Andrew and I talk about these things all the time and he recently told me, "Art is what happens when we have time for something other than basic survival." Weird people have always been the ones who paid attention to the beauty that they felt inside and tried to do something with it after the rock-bottom demands of existence were met. They couldn't help it because, to them, expressing the song of their soul was as critical as food, water, or shelter.

Weird people's place in society eroded slowly at first (then later quite rapidly) as more and more of the creative value was shifted to those who would pour their prodigious energies into designing the conveyor belts, steam engines, time clocks, and all manner of widget producers. Over time, we began to push the offbeat ones to slums and alleys where they could pursue their impractical passions and not represent speed bumps on the path of progress. Whereas they once beautified the human experience and were valued for their work, they became the anachronisms—grit in the gears—and were ignored at best or persecuted and killed at worst.

I have been given the task to redefine the word "weird" and demonstrate that Blessed Weird people are not crazy, hunched-over outcasts who must survive by picking through trash to find crusts of bread discarded by normal people. In fact, we are an honorable tribe with deep, ancient roots, and our time on earth has come.

Throughout the pages of this book, I will use the pronouns "we" and "they" because we will witness examples of those artists-of-life who stand out for how they found what was real in themselves and brought it forth into the world—and find ourselves looking in the mirror they hold up. We will realize that we *are* they and vice versa. Little by little, we will chip away at the barrier between our own everyday selves—the ones who go to work and pay bills and can't find time to create—and those who did it down through history and are doing it right now, today.

In other words, whatever renaissances have happened in the past, we are living right in the middle of a new one—and the greatest of its kind the world has ever seen. You and I have been handed the massive gift and responsibility of a time on earth unlike any that has come before.

We are the richest of all rich kids in the history of the world. Now it is time to do something with all that wealth.

Success in this brave new era does not look like success as it has always been defined before—and neither does failure.

The only success now is living and creating a work-of-art life: unique, rich with meaning, naked of anything we don't care about, and ruthless about carving out something absolutely real from a world that has gorged itself on fakeness and become critically ill from it.

The only failure now is pulling back from that quest because of fear.

In this new renaissance, the highest-value currency is not money or faster machines; it is the ability to see and see and keep seeing the world through different eyes—and then do something with the unique way you see it. That's because the world you saw as a child is not the one we see today. Your ability to rapid-blink, shift perspective, dance forward, sideways, and back as needed, and catch-as-catch-can in a time of tsunami force change has never been more critical.

The new renaissance is loaded with paradox. The world has never been safer and more dangerous, more exciting and soul-strangling boring, stupider and more stunningly intelligent all at the same time than it is at this very moment. This means that the only way to survive the current wave and come out with anything worth having intact is to claim our birthright as creators.

Being creative is the only way we can ever feel fulfilled in life. This means turning our lives into unique works of art that reflect our desires and passions. It also means marching to the beat of our own drum. This book celebrates the weird ones who teach us to do that—who show us that it is not only possible but is also critical to our own survival.

I have this hypothesis about creativity. People who fill the space of their lives with their own creations tend to live longer, have more sex, and actually improve life on this planet without that even necessarily being their agenda. I offer this thought by Anais Nin as Exhibit A in my case: "When you make a world tolerable for yourself, you make a world tolerable for others."

Now it's time to meet the heretics, the rebel magicians, the reluctant heroes, and everyone else in the creative tribe to which you can give yourself permission to belong if you so choose. My purpose in telling their stories (and bits of mine) is to hold up a mirror in which you can meet the gaze of your own genius self and witness the longing in your soul's eyes to express itself with all the color and passion and rebel pleasure that is your truest nature.

Beatitudes for the Weird

Blessed are the weird people
—poets, misfits, writers, mystics
heretics, painters & troubadours—
for they teach us to see the world through different eyes
Blessed are those who embrace the intensity of life's pain and pleasure,
for they shall be rewarded with uncommon ecstasy.
Blessed are ye who see beauty in ugliness,
for you shall transform our vision of how the world might be.
Blessed are the bold and whimsical,
for their imagination shatters ancient boundaries of fear for us all.
Blessed are ye who are mocked for unbridled expression
of love in all its forms,
because your kind of crazy is exactly that freedom
for which the world is unconsciously begging.
Blessed are those who have endured breaking by life,
for they are the resplendent cracks through which the light shines.

CHAPTER
ONE

Listen to Your Heart

I was born with a hole in my heart. A heart murmur. That healed before I started walking upright, but what never changed was a great openness to life that has often left me wondering how it is possible to live in a world that is better suited to those who understand its closed games better than I. In fact, I never felt very savvy or world-wise. I often revealed too much, was too honest, or placed myself in awkward situations that those with more savoir-faire around me would never have risked. It would not surprise me at all to learn that you know exactly what I am talking about.

This is the place where *Blessed Are the Weird* was conceived and born—this confusion of love and beauty and vulnerable, (sometimes crazy) all-in plunges into life. When I first wrote the phrase "blessed are the weird people…" in 2012, I had no idea that the Fates were handing me a drum and that it would become my job to beat it.

So I share these words, which are the drumbeats of my own heart, with those of you who have always seen the world through different eyes and who have the "gift of not fitting in." I write this to you who have a depth of feeling and a not-sureness about exactly how to express it, because you have tried and have often felt misunderstood for your way of being here.

Think of this book as an evolving thumbprint of me, which, if it does its job, will give you a permission slip that you don't really need from anyone (but sometimes still want anyway) to be yourself more deeply than ever. It is also an invitation to trust that your quest to find your place as yourself is not a dead end road.

This is an invitation to come sit with me beside my gypsy campfire out here under the vast sky full of stars. Let's listen to our hearts beating and tell lies that are truer than truth and feel again the electric throb of whatever great creative Force crackles through our veins at times like this. Let's remember the joy of being here and the magic of what might be possible if enough of us are once again free.

From my own wide-broken-open heart to yours, my Blessed Weird tribemates, I offer you this invitation to revive and deepen our commitment to see the world through different eyes. This is our call to live out the vision of how our own worlds might be, and, in so doing, make the whole thing better for everyone.

Where it all begins, I cannot say, this sense of being a stranger in a world full of people who seem to belong in it. All I know is that some of us are not like the others—something in us doesn't fit.

Most of us start to know this in early childhood when we run to our mother or father or a friend with some idea—some way of expressing what we feel—and watch them pull away. Their faces close like shutters, leaving us lonely and afraid that we have done something wrong. We learn to hide and lie about our true selves because what felt like treasure turned out to be dangerous or of little value. These moments are scattered through our childhood, each stealing a piece of our innocence, leaving in its place a wounded patch of flesh now covered in armor. We learn to protect ourselves, to act normal and turn down our light.

We soon find ourselves on a great conveyor belt that carries us into the steel-geared maw of a machine designed to turn us into human widgets. In the classroom and on the playground, we are taught what is valuable and we quickly learn that being curious and sensitive are not rewarded by the teachers or our peers. The ones who get ahead are the savvy ones. They are cool and sharp and hard, like racks of kitchen knives. They are suited to this place, and they slide into their slots as if born to them.

But some of us are awkwardly honest and passionate and interested, tender in odd places, gifted and cursed to feel everything deeply. And yet feeling is power and energy and currency. How we experience life is important. It matters and bears in itself codes and symbols the world needs us to unlock. Who you are, as yourself, is treasure. Those parts of you—the parts that make your insides quiver in case anyone ever saw who you really are—those parts are what the world needs right now.

The bad news is that there is no easy fix for this feeling of otherness that has stuck to our skin like a birthmark for as long as we can remember.

The good news is that learning to embrace this about ourselves is what allows us to find genius in the anomalous beauty of ourselves. In other words, you don't need to undo what makes you different.

As Robert McCammon said in his book, *Boy's Life*:

"When I was twelve years old, the world was my magic lantern, and by its green spirit glow I saw the past, the present, and into the future. You probably did too; you just don't recall it. See, this is my opinion: we all start out knowing magic. We are born with whirlwinds, forest fires, and comets inside us. We are born able to sing to birds and read the clouds and see our destiny in grains of sand. But then we get the magic educated right out of our souls. We get it churched out, spanked out,

washed out, and combed out. We get put on the straight and narrow and told to be responsible. Told to act our age. Told to grow up, for God's sake. And you know why we were told that? Because the people doing the telling were afraid of our wildness and youth, and because the magic we knew made them ashamed and sad of what they'd allowed to wither in themselves."

Children are the weirdest of all humans—before we condition and domesticate them into the norms of society. Go watch a child. Study her. See how she makes expressive faces without any concern about seeming strange or awkward? See how her eyes are wide, wide open to see everything because so much of her world is still new and undefined? Listen as she asks tough, honest questions until some grownup tells her to hush. Watch as she paints the sky of her mind with magic and imagination—how anything and everything is possible still.

Ursula K. Le Guin said, "The creative adult is the child who has survived." That survival is exactly what we are talking about here. We are handed the keys to our own kingdoms again when we recover the tramped-down abilities of the inner child to see and imagine and create.

What's interesting to me about any of us is not how well we can dance like puppets on a string. I only want to know what is real, what is true, and what cannot be ignored. Everything else is a waste of time, which is the same as saying it is a waste of life. There is something that is at once inevitable and at the same time infinitely easy to avoid. That thing is why we are here. It is the North Star that has guided our lives to this point, no matter how far off the path we might have wandered at times. It is the sense of purpose and destiny that wakes us up at night and begs us to pay attention. That thing is the call of Soul.

In every age on earth, there have been people who were not like the others. Strange among their peers, bold in their ideas, always willing to see the world through different eyes, and to do something about the visions that they saw. Restless, colorful, mystical, and disruptive, these people could not be ignored. They were the seers, the storytellers, the dream weavers, the troublemakers, and the heretics. These weird people led insurrections against the forces of stupidity and petrification. Their songs and poems, writings, paintings, parables, and inventions kept the human spirit alive during the darkest ages.

The word "weird" was once "wyrd," which has strong ties to the ideas of fate and destiny. The modern connotation of weird developed from the Middle English use of Weird Sisters for the three Fates or Norns in Norse mythology, the goddesses who controlled human destiny as they cared for great Yggdrasil (the World Tree from which everything springs and correlates with Tree of Life symbols in many other cultures). They were portrayed as odd or frightening in appearance, as in Shakespeare's *Macbeth*, which led to the meaning "odd-looking, uncanny," first used this way around 1815.

The art of living is to fall in love
with life over and over again.
It is no easy thing to walk
through the world
with an open heart,
embracing everything,
and also stand true,
allowing no poison to infect us.
But be cracked open often.
Pour yourself into life
withholding nothing.
Heal and be healed.
This is the way of living in full.

Understood this way, being weird ties in with an ancient sense of destiny. Weird people today are tapping these mythical impulses in our pursuit of what is urgent, irrepressible, and passionate within us—and this, as it turns out, is a destiny quest. We are hearing the long-forgotten whispers of the Fates, who seek to remind us moderns that we, although strange at times, are following the path of our own purpose when we heed these voices.

This whole book is meant as an invitation to embark upon a treasure hunt, because treasure is what we bear within us and there is no greater tragedy than to live and die without ever finding it. But it is not enough to know that we are different or that there were others like us down through the ages of history. What I care about sharing with you is a quest to do something with this knowledge. Otherwise, we can all just nod our heads, say, "...yep, it ain't easy to be me," and slog through the dark swamp of our lives hoping to find a bit of solid ground on which to stand now and then. That's not good enough. We deserve better. We were born in a special era, with important gifts. These gemstones of our nature may be buried under a lot of layers. We may have hidden them from the gaze of the world—and even from ourselves except in the most private moments—but they are worth every bit of the process required to excavate, cut, and polish them into jewels. In fact, the heat and grit and cutting and pressure of this process are necessary because we are not dealing with common stuff here.

It is easy to look at those whose lives seem to glide along on smooth trajectories and wonder what is wrong with us. It is also easy to try to make our feet follow their paths in an effort to be happy and successful like them. There is a problem, though. Every time we do that, we know somewhere deep inside that we have strayed from our own path with heart. No matter how well we might follow someone else's map, something in us silently screams, "You're a fraud!" Nothing is worth that kind of life—not money, not fame, not superficial acceptance. Nothing.

But it is worth everything to live by our own lights and know for sure that we are doing our very own thing in this world. As we do this, we dig into the process of redefining success for ourselves. When this happens, all of our senses become radically alive and engaged. All of those gifts, tools, and perceptions we have hidden before are called into service. We are no longer zombies shuffling along to the collective drumbeat. Now we are animated, soulful, and dynamically collaborating with the universe to create our destiny.

As we look backward in time and learn about the others who marched off the beaten path with a scythe and blazed a new trail, we gain courage to do likewise. Because we, the Blessed Weird People, are our own sort of tribe, flung across the span of history like a loose web. Now the web is tightening. We are finding each other, and as we do, we are granted vision and strength to keep at the process of becoming real—of becoming ourselves.

Speaking of our predecessors for a moment, I really didn't know what I was doing when I first wrote the words that started this thing several years ago. They just happened, born from my own sense of longing and confusion about how to navigate life in this world.

Blessed are the weird people...
Poets, misfits, writers, mystics, heretics,
Painters, and troubadours...
For they teach us to see the world through different eyes.

At the time, I didn't know why that troupe of characters showed up on the page. I only knew that somehow I was speaking for myself and everyone who has ever felt out of place but sure that they had something to offer the world if they could just find a way to do it.

In the few years since that time, millions of people around the world have taken up this little saying like a battle cry. It surprised me to discover that there are so many of us here who feel this way. I felt so alone before. If this book does its job, it will help us all see how we are part of a long and honorable heritage of weird people who made great contributions to the human story. It will help us understand that we are not alone in our quest to make something real and valuable of our lives. I can hear the ghost of great painter and creative rebel Frida Kahlo whispering to us all, "*I used to think I was the strangest person in the world, but then I thought there are so many people in the world, there must be someone just like me who feels bizarre and flawed in the same ways I do. I would imagine her, and imagine that she must be out there thinking of me too. Well, I hope that if you are out there and read this and know that, yes, it's true I'm here, and I'm just as strange as you.*"

You are not alone.

Oriah Mountain Dreamer, my dear friend and author of the powerful book, *The Invitation*, said, "*All dreamers and poets are pirates navigating by the stars, raiding the private places of inner worlds for the gold hidden there.*"

I'll introduce these artists, leaders, and troublemakers in a moment, but before I do, I need to say that most of us are living the creative archetypes—either consciously or unconsciously. The musicians, writers, heretics, painters, mystics, and troubadours of all times are alive within us, struggling to break free.

This was the case for me. I could feel the kicking of unborn creative impulses in me as a child, forcing me into art and reading and music, singing and dreaming. I took painting lessons, drew constantly, learned the violin, played in an orchestra, acted in school plays, and sang in a traveling gospel quartet. Nothing quite stuck and I felt frustrated most of the time because this "something" was pushing and drumming against the inside of my rib cage. It wouldn't show itself in a way that I could recognize—no distinct outline I could identify—so I forced myself out into the world and took on roles that didn't suit me well but allowed me to pour all that energy into something tangible at least. I became a salesman and worked jobs for Coca Cola and cell phone companies. I worked in the lower intestines of the financial industry for years and started a mortgage company that, for a while, provided a creative outlet as I designed sales teams, built offices, and wrote business plans for an empire I hoped would answer my own deep questions about "why am I here?"

But it wasn't working. I wasn't happy. My soul wasn't saying "yes" to the life I had created, but I had no idea what to do about it.

There was something true, something "me" that I wasn't able to get out. One of my favorite writers as an early teen was L.M. Montgomery. What she said describes my experience of entering the world almost perfectly:

"I grew up out of that strange, dreamy childhood of mine and went into the world of reality. I met with experiences that bruised my spirit - but they never harmed my ideal world. That was always mine to retreat into at will. I learned that that world and the real world clashed hopelessly and irreconcilably; and I learned to keep them apart so that the former might remain for me unspoiled. I learned to meet other people on their own ground since there seemed to be no meeting place on mine. I learned to hide the thoughts and dreams and fancies that had no place in the strife and clash of the market place. I found that it was useless to look for kindred souls in the multitude; one might stumble on such here and there, but as a rule, it seemed to me that the majority of people lived for the things of time and sense alone and could not understand my other life. So I piped and danced to other people's piping - and held fast to my own soul as best I could."

"...and held fast to my own soul as best I could."

There were many times I felt lost and afraid that the confusing voices of the world "out there" and the struggling, urgent mass of what was trying to find its way out from within would never make peace with each other.

My heart reaches out to embrace all of us who deal with the confusing tension of the call to a renaissance life. We are not one thing. We are not one person. We are many and all at the same time. Life is not simple or straightforward for those of us who must fight to express the many truths of who we are in a world that says, "Just pick something and do it." And you will do it, but not before you have realized that you are a diamond of many facets. You have the energy to shine in multiple ways and that shining eventually becomes a unified, sparkling expression of yourself.

This is massively liberating.

Relax into this understanding—nothing is wasted. All of your experiences, all of the broken pieces of relationships and half-formed careers, everything you are and have been—it may appear to be a basket of dusty shards, but come with me now and meet other creators so you can see that, somehow, every jagged little piece of you will find its place in a kaleidoscope of brilliance if you stay with the task of becoming yourself.

And …

That is the only mission great enough to be worthy of who you really are.

CHAPTER
TWO

The Poets

> *"Poetry is a life-cherishing force.*
> *For poems are not words, after all, but fires for the cold, ropes let*
> *down to the lost, something as necessary as bread*
> *in the pockets of the hungry."*
> — Mary Oliver

Poets and poetry have little place in our practical, linear lives. Most moderns don't have time to decipher the sensuous language of the bards. Poetry doesn't make sense to the rational mind and it's not supposed to. That doesn't diminish the fact that some buried part of us remembers and yearns for this ancient form of communication.

Poetry may have come before our ability to read and write. Historians believe that the earliest poetry was recited or sung— passed down from generation to generation of teacher-poets who helped their tribes remember oral history, genealogy, and law. It is hard to separate poetry from musical traditions, and most of the most ancient poems were, in fact, hymns. Early poets also passed down stories of historical events, love songs, fiction, and even instructions for the proper carrying-out of everyday tasks.

Scholars discovered the work of Sumerian priestess Enheduanna, who was among the first of all women in recorded history to have her name remembered for posterity. She was the powerful priestess-princess in the Sumerian city-state of Ur, daughter of king Sargon. She composed at least forty-two hymns, which were addressed to temples in the known world of that time. In them, she said, "My king, something has been created that no one has created before." No one, as far as the historians can tell, had recorded poetry in permanent form before that time, but her hymns to the goddess Inanna were carved into stone tablets and became the first attempt at a systematic theology.

Hindu poets composed the Vedas and Upanishads somewhere between 1700-1200 BCE, and Homer famously wrote his Iliad and Odyssey in the era of 800-675 BCE. These epic poems yield many clues about the state of the world, the cosmology of the ancients, and the ambitions of humankind as a whole during times nearly buried in the sands of history. Poetry also appears among the earliest records of most literate cultures, with poetic fragments found on monoliths, rune stones, and stelae.

In other words, poets were a big deal for a very long time. Poetry's power in society eroded when our lifestyles and ambitions became more and more focused on mechanical outcomes. As we built machines to make life predictable, we lost interest in the symbolic language of poetry and we stopped paying poets to teach us in this way. Because of the relentless pressures of a dawning Industrial Age, we stopped wanting to know the unknowable in favor of the harsh, calloused literalness of what science can measure in our pragmatic world.

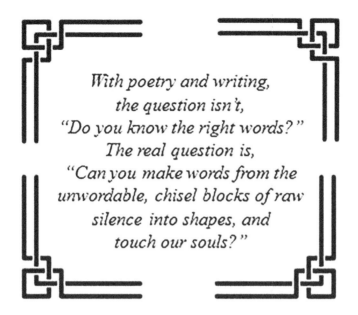

With poetry and writing,
the question isn't,
"Do you know the right words?"
The real question is,
"Can you make words from the
unwordable, chisel blocks of raw
silence into shapes, and
touch our souls?"

Poets have been wording the unwordable for us long before we knew how to turn their heart murmurings into books and sell them. They have been translating what the soul has to say in its strange, coded way into something we can remember—into something we can feel. The information they give us takes the form of lyrical downloads that we might receive as school children and never unzip themselves within us until some perfect moment during adulthood when we need them most. Just because it has become harder for poets to earn a living doesn't mean that the spark of divine madness has been extinguished, though.

Like the troubadours, about whom we will talk later, poets were often called upon to conceal the literal truths they were trying to share under layers of soft language. Sometimes we can find clues and hidden meanings in their lines that surprise us in this day of relative freedom of speech. It doesn't make sense why they needed to shroud everything the way they did, but when we remember that if they wrote what they really wanted to say in direct language, they might get roasted at the stake, so we can feel their secret glee at slipping a dose of truth into the spoonful of jammy words that disguised the medicine.

Poet and novelist Babette Deutsch said, *"Poetry is the fiery index to the genius of the age."* Yes, a fiery index, revealing things brought back from the ragged forward edge of what is happening in a particular time, distilling them into words laden with feeling. Poetry is zeitgeist. Poets tell us truths that the authorities of the day have not caught up with yet.

Often as not, though, I suspect they didn't know what they were doing. The great soul of the world needed to say something and it caught their heart's eye with the flutter of a bird's wing, or the way the sun painted a tree trunk golden just before nightfall, or the aching thud of emptiness left behind after the loss of a love. They probably didn't even know that they were mouthpieces of Something that must express itself and needed to find a human to do it.

At the beginning of this chapter I quoted Mary Oliver, one of my favorite modern poets, and I love how she describes this work: *"Poetry is a life-cherishing force. For poems are not words, after all, but fires for the cold, ropes let down to the lost, something as necessary as bread in the pockets of the hungry."*

"…a life cherishing force."

"…fires for the cold."

"…ropes let down to the lost."

The poets who touch our souls so precisely with words bathed in feeling do that for us. They help us see the world through different eyes. They write lines of emotional code that bypass our minds and speak to that nameless longing in us. They help us remember who we really are and what we desire most. They help us feel our lives again. As Arti Honrao said, *"I do not write poetry; I take words and dip them in feelings."*

Since I'm being horribly honest, I'll tell you that I don't like

Shakespeare or Wordsworth much, but there are others whose words hit me dead center at perfect moments in my life.

Ginsberg's "Howl" with its profane and sacred madness sweeps me into a mystical experience of life at times when I have forgotten.

"...Holy! Holy! Holy! Holy! Holy! Holy! Holy! Holy! Holy!
Holy! Holy! Holy! Holy! Holy! Holy!
The world is holy! The soul is holy! The skin is holy!
The nose is holy! The tongue and cock and hand
and asshole holy!
Everything is holy! Everybody's holy! Everywhere is
holy! Everyday is in eternity! Everyman's an angel!
The bum's as holy as the seraphim! The madman is
holy as you my soul are holy!
The typewriter is holy the poem is holy the voice is
holy the hearers are holy the ecstasy is holy!..."

Anaïs Nin seduces me into raw truth and beauty and courage.

"And the day came when the risk to remain tight in a bud was more painful than the risk it took to blossom."

Hafiz tells me who the poets are and what they do.

"A poet is someone who can pour light into a cup, then raise it to nourish your beautiful parched holy mouth."

Sometimes that wild man, Walt Whitman, drags me from behind my desk and commands me to live and dance—naked, hairy, and primal.

"I too am not a bit tamed, I too am untranslatable,

I sound my barbaric yawp over the roofs of the world."

Hafiz comes back to say it in a way that I can never ignore.

"I am a hole in the flute through which the Christ's breath moves. Listen to this music."

He expresses this surrender to feeling, to a super-mind knowing, to universal truth and rapture that begs us also to be a hole in the flute and allow the eternal, mysterious breath of All to move through the space of our lives and make music with our existence.

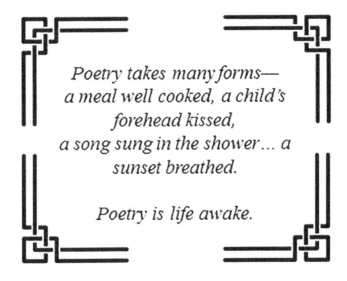

*Poetry takes many forms—
a meal well cooked, a child's
forehead kissed,
a song sung in the shower... a
sunset breathed.*

Poetry is life awake.

Whether or not we think of ourselves as poets or even poetry lovers, the fact remains that the spirits of those primitive teacher-artists are alive in in our blood and bones. We thrill to the sound of their words at times when our souls are hungry. We need them to have their strange way of seeing things, to make up words when no others can describe what they feel, and to share the gifts of their weirdly gorgeous souls with us. They help us remember to live.

And, through my eyes, poetry is never just words on paper. It's a way of seeing, feeling, and expressing life itself.

A few days ago, I woke up early and took a road trip to Sun Valley, Idaho. The road was dark when I started, but I cruised straight into the dawn as it rose from behind the mountains. I was going to meet my friend Chris Grosso at the famous Sun Valley Wellness Festival, where he was a featured speaker. I drove along, sipping coffee and listening to Jack Kerouac's *Big Sur* while the sun's early light painted the world around me with bright colors.

I had been feeling numb for several weeks—insulated from myself and from the deep sensations of life that I cherish. I fear numbness. My raw senses that receive all the nuanced vibrations are not just icing on the cake for me. They are the whole cake, the plate, the table, and the music too. If I can't feel, I can't access what for me is the most vital fuel of existence.

Overhead, ravens appeared at different times, leading the way into the mountains. Late spring rains had left shallow ponds that reflected the sunrise, and wildflowers created skiffs of color under the ancient gaze of hills that still retained a bit of winter's snow. I felt my spirit come alive and knew that somehow this day was exactly what I had been unconsciously begging for.

I arrived at the Sun Valley Inn and found my seat in the conference room where David Whyte was set to speak. His talk was titled "What to Remember When Waking," which is also the title of one of his poems. I have been aware of Whyte for a few years but had never explored his work much. What I had read told me that I must not miss this great philosopher-poet's talk.

After another twenty minutes, the master of ceremonies gave a few words and introduced him. David Whyte stumped up the stairs and took the stage in his brown canvas pants stuffed into rustic-looking leather boots. He appeared to have come straight in from a solitary walk through the moors.

When he began to speak, my spirit said an old, familiar "yesss." His voice carried the rich twists of a Welsh-Irish ancestry and he had about him the air of someone well lived and comfortable with himself—much like the boots he wore. He told stories colored with highland lakes, and heartbreak, and pints of ale in smoky pubs; with living and loving. The first poem he shared was a selection from Wordsworth. As I have said, I'm not terribly fond of the classical poets, but he made those ten lines come alive for me. It wasn't the words so much as how he connected the web of soul in them to my own soul and to all of this life that we share.

Halfway through, tears were running down my face. They were tears of remembering. Tears of relief. Tears of reawakening. David Whyte stood there as a living signpost pointing the way back home to myself. He reminded me that a poet can also be a grounded teacher with real work in this modern world that is so hungry to reclaim its soul.

After I returned home, I visited his website and found what he wrote about poetry and poets.

"The poet lives and writes at the frontier between deep internal experience and the revelations of the outer world. There is no going back once this frontier has been reached; a new territory is visible and what has been said cannot be unsaid. The discipline of poetry is in overhearing yourself say difficult truths from which it is impossible to retreat.

Poetry is a break for freedom. In a sense, all poems are good; all poems are an emblem of courage and the attempt to say the unsayable, but only a few are able to speak to something universal yet personal and distinct at the same time; to create a door through which others can walk into what previously seemed unobtainable realms, in the passage of a few short lines."

Remembering Life
Jacob Nordby

"Hello," says Life. "Remember me?
We started out together here
When you were just
a bundle of amazement.
Remember how you saw the world
With nothing but wonder?
We were such rowdy playmates then.
We painted on the sky with clouds
And made magic out of
Clothespins and peanut butter.
Remember, can you, how I became
stained and heavy
With trouble?
Not safe now. So much no.
They dressed me in painful clothes
And made you wear them, too.
You don't recognize me, do you?
But I've never abandoned you
Or lost my wild, happy desire
To show you
Play with you
Kiss you
Hide and seek down twisty paths
And always discover more.
Want to run away with me again?

Shall we elope without ever leaving
Because that's possible, you know.
I've never been anywhere but here
Waiting for you
To remember."

CHAPTER
THREE

The Misfits

*"Here's to the crazy ones. The misfits. The rebels. The troublemakers.
The round pegs in the square holes. The ones who see things
differently. They're not fond of rules, and they have no respect for the
status quo. You can quote them; disagree with them; glorify or vilify
them. About the only thing you can't do is ignore them. Because they
change things. They push the human race forward. And while some
may see them as the crazy ones, we see genius. Because the people who
are crazy enough to think they can change the world are
the ones who do."*

\- Rob Siltanen

I think it's funny to quote Apple Computer's "Think Different"
ad script in this book. I wish like hell that I could attribute this
excerpt to Jack Kerouac as others have done. He is a much more
romantic character in the gypsy vanguard and seems to be the
antithesis of corporate marketing shills cranking out ad copy to sell
computers. But I'm reminded of what famous author Neil Gaiman,
an exquisitely weird guy in his own right, said. "The art isn't the artist,
the poem isn't the poet; trust the tale, not the teller."

And, since we're bringing in the ad guys for a minute, here's what

David Ogilvy had to say: "Talent, I believe, is most likely to be found among nonconformists, dissenters, and rebels."

As we look at the misfits now, it is good to fix that in our minds. We have a perfectionist's tendency to put artists, writers, musicians, and the like on pedestals. We might be living "lives of quiet desperation"—grinding along behind desks, selling our time to keep the bills paid—but we expect real creatives to remain pure and never sell out. That is a double standard and it keeps many of us from ever going there for ourselves because we assume that we don't have what it takes or can't remain unsullied enough to produce something so fine. In other words, if we have art, poems, music, inventions, or tales to be told in us, we need to trust them and where they come from rather than getting hung up on our own lack of trustworthiness as creatives. It is only this belief in our own possible insincerity that blocks us from going on the great archaeological mission to unearth what is real within. We all have some absolutely unique components that do not fit the life or the culture into which we have been domesticated. Even if we are living what appear to be the most vanilla existences, somewhere in there is gold—that slightly-off, anomalous genius that would yield enormous benefits if only we would not hide it. No matter how good we are at fitting in, if we care enough, we can find our inner misfit.

Fear is the only thing that keeps us from it.

In my first attempt at a novel, *The Divine Arsonist - A Tale of Awakening*, one of the supernatural Helpers told the main character (whose life closely resembled my own in many ways):

"You were given the gift of not fitting in. You'll learn much more about this later, but you will come to know that you were given the ability to see things differently from other people. The price you paid feels high, but you'll soon understand that it was worth every moment.

By the way, most people don't realize that the most precious gifts in life come hidden inside of painful wrapping paper."

Had you met me ten or twelve years ago, you would not have been able to pick me out of any lineup of thirty-something, upwardly mobile men. I was domesticated top to bottom, from haircut to shoes. I had the right house, my business card listed important titles, I was well regarded in the community, and even my then-mother-in-law didn't think I was a bad person. I was an expert at standing in line. You wouldn't have thought I possessed an inner misfit. I had always been an A student in school and never caused my parents trouble. I was a boring, normal, nice guy. The problem was, I knew better and I felt like a fraud inside that respectable outfit.

Growing up, I was awkward, insecure, and naïve. I felt that most people knew something I didn't about life. Paradoxically, I had this secret conviction that I had a special mission in the world—I just had no idea what it was or how to find it. No matter how hard I tried to fit in, I always ended up silently cursing myself after being with people because I was sure they could see through my attempts to make easy small talk and sound smart like the others. Rather than explore the nature of my unique gifts, I spent all my energy working hard to be like other people so that maybe they would let me stay. It was a lot like wearing an ill-fitting suit of armor. It kept out the arrows most of the time, but it was heavy and restrictive, and always clanked or squeaked at the wrong moments.

We all know some people who act out in socially awkward or unacceptable ways and then make a big deal about the fact that they are "…just so different that no one understands them." This isn't what I'm talking about. That's the same as trying to be weird for weird's sake. It amounts to a cry for help, but isn't authentic and it doesn't gain them what they really want—acceptance by some group. The pathetic thing about this is that these people usually don't care which group accepts them. They will change colors as often as necessary, never realizing that they must discover who they really are and accept themselves before anyone else can. If you have the gift of not fitting in, rather than flaunting it, more likely you have tried to cover it up your whole life.

Throughout history, the misfits we remember struggled mightily and eventually came to a point where the only honest thing they could do was be themselves in all their awkward, bumpy glory. When this watershed moment arrived, they chose to live by their own lights and we remember them as heroes because of it.

One of the primary archetypes in many legends is the Reluctant Hero. A reluctant hero is an ordinary man or woman—usually with a great wound or chaotic past that makes them resistant to any idea that they might be worthy to perform acts of heroism or service. During the tale, they are called into action against their protests. They rise to the occasion, and although they are often beaten and bloody by the story's end, they avenge a wrong or vanquish a foe. They often deal with inner demons, weaknesses, and doubts about whether or not they will succeed in their mission. Their misgivings, insecurities, and general ordinariness allow us to identify with them and believe that perhaps we, too, might be heroes-in-waiting.

Misfits who accept their gift of not fitting in are the ones who use the tension and loneliness to forge something magnificent. They inspire us to rise above our mundane and painfully ordinary circumstances to achieve the extraordinary in our lives. This is why we love the stories of Moses from the Old Testament, Neo in *The Matrix*, Frodo Baggins in *Lord of the Rings*, Katniss Everdeen in *The Hunger Games*, Harry Potter, and many others, both ancient and modern. We see ourselves in their reflection and we thrill to imagine that we might overcome the odds despite our personal weaknesses; that we might return home bearing victory and healing. We are also given hope that, after we have emerged from the chaos, we will be seen and accepted for who we are—not because we kept our heads down and blended into the scenery.

I love what Stephen Fry has to say about this —

"I have always felt separate… I have always felt unable to join in, to let go, to become part of the tribe. I have always sniped or joked from the sidelines. I have never, ever, lost my overwhelmingly self-conscious self-consciousness.

"It's not all bad. Heightened self-consciousness, apartness, an inability to join in, physical shame, and self-loathing—they are not all bad. Those devils have also been my angels. Without them, I would never have disappeared into language, literature, the mind, laughter, and all the mad intensities that made and unmade me."

Of course, not everyone will rise to the occasion. Those who fall into victimhood and depression simply lie alongside the path like cautionary skeletons. But failure is not what we are here to talk about. We are here to reclaim what makes us unique and powerful. We are here to learn how to love ourselves and leverage our gifts into a victory so satisfying and personal that we will outstrip the doubts about whether or not we were ever worthy.

There's another group that must not be ignored under the heading of Misfits—the comedians. It's easy to see these people as nothing more than shock jocks. They often stand up there on stage and curse and smoke and drink and say horrible, true things that make us laugh. We sometimes look around guiltily and hope no one notices us snickering at their antics, but they come from a lineage that kings and rulers relied upon to tell the truth wrapped in laughter. Jesters were not just happy idiots prancing about for the amusement of royal courts. They were given nearly complete immunity to say whatever they needed to, even if it would have been a hanging or beheading offense coming from anyone else.

Bon vivant Irish author, playwright, and poet Oscar Wilde said,

"If you want to tell people the truth, make them laugh. Otherwise, they'll kill you."

This misfit truth-telling role of comedians is so deeply entrenched in our consciousness that it occupies its own archetype—The Fool. You will even find a tarot card dedicated to the Jester or Fool. It is an important card in the deck and some interpret the childlike curiosity of the sign to indicate new beginnings or different approaches.

I sometimes enjoy rattling my own sensibilities by watching a Bill Hicks comedy special. He was dark and raw, but he also told many truths and even shared transcendent universal wisdom at times. Right in the middle of a frantic rant with cigarette smoke curling around his head, he would say something like *"This is where we are right now, as a whole. No one is left out of the loop. We are experiencing a reality based on a thin veneer of lies and illusions. A world where greed is our God and wisdom is sin, where division is key and unity is fantasy, where the ego-driven cleverness of the mind is praised, rather than the intelligence of the heart."* He criticized the war on drugs, our national pride, the corrosive influence of television, oppressive religious beliefs, and many other things that make us squirm at the same time as we are laughing.

Then there's Russell Brand. He embodies the Jester archetype like no one else I have seen. He's brash, he's egotistical; he boasts about his messiah complex and his massive sex appeal—but he manages to blend these in an electric cocktail of razor-sharp humor, raw admission of his own foibles, and the kind of lovable hubris that almost no one else could get away with.

When he turns his attention to the current state of affairs and our leaders, he makes "the way things are" seem pitiful and stupid. I have watched him on major television shows as he turns the program upside down and leaves the hosts gasping for air. He appeared before the British Parliament shirtless beneath his leather vest, hair hanging around his shoulders with rock star negligence. He explained exactly why he feels that the way we handle drug addiction is compounding the problem exponentially and exposed the corporations who collude with governments to keep the entire wheel of pain turning.

Russell has proclaimed himself the leader of a revolution. It's hard to take him seriously, skipping around the stage in high-heeled boots and tight leather pants, but he is impossible to ignore. His ideas are so fresh and bold and ultimately sane that I can't dismiss him as just another attention whore—even though he is that and admits it without missing a single beat.

Archimedes famously said, "Give me a place on which to stand and with a lever I shall move the world." Russell Brand wants to use his singular celebrity as a platform from which to do just that. Yes, he is just one court jester cutting up antics in the halls of the powerful, but he has the ears and hearts of millions of young people who are not content to live in and recreate the same kind of world that their parents have.

Comedians get a special hall pass for this kind of subversiveness because they occupy a place in society that allows us to pretend that we aren't taking them seriously. They can say anything about anyone and not get sent to prison. That's their job, just as it was the job of court jesters centuries ago. They are dark, they are neurotic, they are batshit crazy—and they sometimes tell us truth we need to hear in ways that no one else can. At the very least, they hold up a mirror so society can see its own absurd and often ugly reflection.

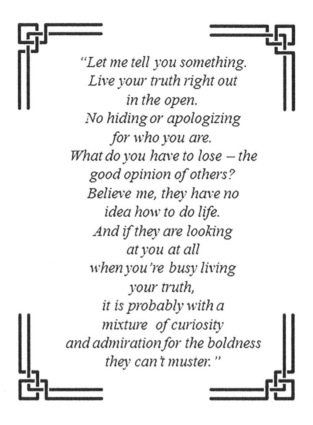

"*Let me tell you something.*
Live your truth right out
in the open.
No hiding or apologizing
for who you are.
What do you have to lose – the
good opinion of others?
Believe me, they have no
idea how to do life.
And if they are looking
at you at all
when you're busy living
your truth,
it is probably with a
mixture of curiosity
and admiration for the boldness
they can't muster."

Misfits come in many shapes and not all of them are easy to deal with. We don't know how to handle people whose minds are bent or cracked. There's that thin line of mad genius in many of them that makes us want to pay attention but also triggers revulsion in us. They get under our skin and disturb our smooth lives. They are often inconvenient people to have around. My heart aches for people who deal with ADHD, Asperger's, autism, bi-polar disorder, schizophrenia, or other socially difficult conditions. If anyone should ever get the green light for feeling like a victim of fate or genetics, someone who suffers from one or more of these things seems to qualify. But look at this list of people who have delighted us and made the world a better place in spite of (and probably because of) their misfit ways:

- Abraham Lincoln
- Agatha Christie
- Axl Rose
- Buzz Aldrin
- Drew Carey
- Edgar Allan Poe
- Hans Christian Andersen
- Isaac Newton
- Jim Carey
- Jimi Hendrix
- Kurt Cobain
- Liz Taylor
- Ludwig Van Beethoven
- Mark Twain
- Mel Gibson
- Ozzy Osbourne
- Plato
- Ralph Waldo Emerson
- Robert Downey, Jr.
- Robin Williams
- Sinead O'Connor
- Stephen Fry
- Tim Burton
- Vincent Van Gogh
- Virginia Woolf
- Winston Churchill
- Wolfgang Amadeus Mozart

…and many others

Each of these extraordinary people had what some might call mental problems, but they managed to allow the brilliant shards in their minds to fall into place like pieces of broken glass in a kaleidoscope and create something beautiful, something fascinating, or something that changed the course of human history.

Now we just medicate these people. We numb them out and dull the sharp edges of the cracks in their minds. It's important to know that what many have said is wrong with them might be that "gift of not fitting in" that is exactly right with them. I'm not suggesting that people should refuse professional help when it is needed, but I am saying that we need to stop allowing ourselves to be pressed down into a homogenous mold in the name of making everyone comfortable until we lose that spark of something different in ourselves.

The main thing is that we stop trying so hard to be at home in a culture that seems to have little patience for us and at last come home to ourselves. When this happens, we are no longer misfits. We are heroes—reluctant about it to be sure, but heroes nonetheless because we have taken the road less traveled and found our own treasure.

I saw a funny couch pillow the other day. It was cross-stitched in old-fashioned style with the words *"Behold the field in which I grow my fucks and see that it is barren."* It made me laugh and it also made me think. We place people who seem to lack any concern about the opinions of other people on a pedestal. They seem so rugged and free and awesome.

They also are not real.

The truth is, everyone (except for sociopaths) cares about what other people think. We all care to some degree or another, and we should not be ashamed of ourselves for this. It is, however, a great liberation to learn that other people are mostly not thinking about us at all, and that we can go about our own business of living without first calibrating every action against whether or not "they" will like it.

But we do need people and to suggest otherwise is thrice-distilled hubris. The trick is learning how to become interdependent and jettison the sick co-dependent coping strategies.

The trouble with living by our own lights and blazing our own trails is that we often feel lonely. Since we are tribal creatures, this is one of those fears with ancient roots. To be isolated from the tribe often meant death. Weird people are especially susceptible to feeling alone in the world. The early sense of "I am not like the others" can become excruciating over time as we strive to fit in but so frequently fail.

Many people overcompensate for this by pretending as if they don't care at all. They act out in all sorts of strange ways under some declaration like, "I just do my own thing." But what they really want is acceptance.

Acceptance.

We all crave that. It is the same thing as the feeling of being at home—home in the best way, home if home were the safest place on earth and no one would ever put us down or make us feel like strangers there. Now we are talking about one of the most basic of all human needs. The sad truth is that many of us never felt safe or accepted even in our own homes. We were imprinted from earliest memory with the sense of not belonging. This often leads to a lifetime of fear and struggle in which we walk through the world contorting ourselves in a desperate attempt to show that we do fit—that we can belong. It holds us back from ever standing straight and showing up as ourselves.

Since I wished I could quote Jack Kerouac at the beginning of this chapter, I'll do it now. This is one of my favorite clips from his book, *On the Road*. It describes the passionate misfit spirit, even though many of us are more reserved personalities than this might suggest.

"...the only people for me are the mad ones, the ones who are mad to live, mad to talk, mad to be saved, desirous of everything at the same time, the ones who never yawn or say a commonplace thing, but burn, burn, burn, like fabulous yellow roman candles exploding like spiders across the stars and in the middle you see the blue centerlight pop and everybody goes 'Awww!'"

CHAPTER FOUR

The Writers

*"How many a man has dated a new era in his life
from the reading of a book."*
– Henry David Thoreau

Writers are magicians. They pull ideas from the sky and turn them into marks on paper that enter our minds and change our lives. Some writers deny the power of sorcery available to them and choose to regurgitate a stream of refried collective ideas or a thinly disguised batch of propaganda, but I'm talking about the ones who are able to straddle two worlds and make words come to life. They lead us into epic, fantastic journeys. They get behind our defenses and reveal our deepest fears, our dreams, and our soul desires. They lead us to the razor's edge of watershed decisions and show us it is possible to follow our hearts.

The writers I'm talking about are weird people.

Maybe, like me, the sky of your childhood imagination was painted by L.M. Montgomery, Charles Dickens, Louisa May Alcott, Gene Stratton Porter, Herman Melville, C.S. Lewis, J.R.R. Tolkien, Alexandre Dumas, and others?

Perhaps later you found Ernest Hemingway and John Steinbeck

and Paulo Coelho and Ken Kesey and Neil Gaiman and Jack Kerouac? Were they pied pipers who knew exactly which tune to play so you would slip the strictures of your world and follow them into magical places from which you would never fully return?

Did they take you to mountain peaks for a few hours from which you could see the whole, vast, expansive world—even if the smaller one you lived in was repressive and dull?

I don't use the words "magic" or "magical" lightly.

Writers' ability to commune with the muses and transcribe what those invisible guides have to say is no small matter. It is a special kind of sorcery. Writers have been admired and feared for as long as any of us can remember. It makes little sense, though. Anyone can stand up and say, "I'm a writer." Then they can sit down and write whatever kind of crazy shit they want. That shouldn't pose a threat to anyone. It does, though. Writers have always led us beyond the reality we currently inhabit. They have showed us things we hadn't yet imagined were possible. They posed questions—subtle, sneaky questions woven into stories—that found their way past our conditioned minds and burrowed into our hearts. These became seeds that sprouted and grew into something transcendent.

Have you ever read a book, which, after you finished the last page, left you feeling dizzy and a little disoriented when you walked out into the everyday world again?

I have.

When I first read Thoreau's words "...*many a man has dated a new era in his life from the reading of a book*," I said an audible "yes!" That has happened to me more than once. Writers have spoken to me from where they sit on their perches down through the generations and said things that could never be unsaid. They asked me questions that would never again be unasked. They rang bells in my soul that could not be unrung.

Their propensity for doing that has always made writers

dangerous to the status quo. Something happens when an honest, inquisitive man or woman sits down to write. It's mysterious. They tap into the collective soul, the unconscious, and super-conscious all at the same time—at least the weird ones do. They say things everyone wants and needs to say, but for which no one else can find words. We all need them to do this. Without people who are willing to follow imagination beyond the edge of what is currently possible, we can't move forward. The trouble with this is that it shakes the foundations of what-already-is and disturbs the comfortable power of those who control it. Why else would the novel *Satanic Verses*—a work of fiction, mind you—by Salman Rushdie infuriate the then Supreme Leader of Iran, Ayatollah Khomeini, enough to issue a *fatwā* calling for his death?

History is full of writers who refused to color inside the lines of their time. Ever since humans can remember having such things as books, scrolls, or clay tablets, writers have been misbehaving. After they have had their solitary fun and someone lets the word out about the mischief they created all by themselves, the bureaucrats come marching in to make a pile of their books and set fire to them. Since most of the townspeople owe their next meal to the powers that be in some way, they all stand around and applaud this barbarity.

I will say, though, that it's a rare writer who makes history and means to cause this kind of havoc. Best I can tell (and with some notable exceptions), most are introverted types and say what they must because they can't help it. It is as if the wing-footed messenger god Hermes is moving their pens and they are following along as best they can. We need them to keep doing this. Without them, we would be unimaginably stuck in the mud as a race.

Every once in a while, some writer comes along and puts down a few sentences of such perfection that makes us all stand back and take a collective breath. I will never forget reading this from Ernest Hemingway's *A Farewell to Arms*:

"*That night at the hotel, in our room with the long empty hall outside and our shoes outside the door, a thick carpet on the floor of the room, outside the windows the rain falling and in the room light and pleasant and cheerful, then the light out and it exciting with smooth sheets and the bed comfortable, feeling that we had come home, feeling no longer alone, waking in the night to find the other one there, and not gone away; all other things were unreal. We slept when we were tired and if we woke the other one woke too so one was not alone. Often a man wishes to be alone and a girl wishes to be alone too and if they love each other they are jealous of that in each other, but I can truly say we never felt that. We could feel alone when we were together, alone against the others ... But we were never lonely and never afraid when we were together. I know that the night is not the same as the day: that all things are different, that the things of the night cannot be explained in the day, because they do not then exist, and the night can be a dreadful time for lonely people once their loneliness has started. But with Catherine there was almost no difference in the night except that it was an even better time. If people bring so much courage to the world the world has to kill them to break them, so of course it kills them. The world breaks every one and afterward many are strong at the broken places. But those that will not break it kills. It kills the very good and the very gentle and the very brave impartially. If you are none of these you can be sure it will kill you too but there will be no special hurry.*"

Most of us have seen "*...the world breaks every one and afterward many are strong at the broken places*" quoted, but that bit leaves out the love and longing and soul-cracking pathos of the rest of it. Hemingway found a way to capture all of that in a single paragraph. That's why we love him. It's also why we love any artist—poet, songwriter, or painter—who can show us what we feel but don't know how to express it.

There is a strong chance that you are one of these writers, just as you may fit into others of the Weird People categories. When I began writing, I learned how difficult it was to step forward and offer the world what came through me. In the act of writing, I often imagined that I could feel the spirits of Hemingway, Steinbeck, Twain, and others leaning over my shoulders, watching every word as it appeared on the screen. That might sound like august company to keep, but it was a lot of pressure. My admiration for their work made me keenly aware of what I was up to and how unqualified I felt to perform on their stage.

The time came when I realized that probably none of them knew what they were doing when they were doing it either. They may have mastered certain tools of style, but the act of writing must be approached naked if it is going to have any life in it.

It's the same for us too. Nothing we have created before will help us do another authentic thing if we can't silence our own misgivings and ego. The Muse invites us to step into that space that allows us to weave something visible from all the invisible scraps and threads of imagination that are attracted to the magnetic pull of such an act. Writers are weird. The whole process is weird and if we are willing to strip completely naked, bow to Hermes and the muses, and begin to write with no guarantees that anything worthy will come of our efforts, it is just possible that we can offer the world something it needs us to say.

Hemingway once wrote, *"You must be prepared to work always without applause."* I am in that very balancing-act state as I write these words. I cannot know whether any of this will survive the editor's pen to meet your eyes. I do not know whether it is any good or can be made to make sense in the end. I admit that now because by the time you hold this book in your hands, it might be easy to assume that I (and others like me who get their books written and published) don't struggle with the same self-doubt and inner critic that stops so many from expressing what is in them. But we all do, (except the very arrogant and stupid who seem to have a bottomless well of unfounded confidence that their voices are worth hearing) and this very struggle with ourselves and the world and everything is what makes every single creation that survives these fires ... priceless in the same way that every baby who survives birth is.

CHAPTER
FIVE

The Mystics

"Sell your cleverness and buy bewilderment."
– Rumi

Now we wade into the deep end of the pool with the likes of Lao Tzu, Buddha, Hafiz, Jesus Christ, Meister Eckhart, Carlos Castaneda, and many others. This is not a sociable group of skinny dippers. They are all so quiet and tend to float off into solitary corners and stare at the sky.

It is hard to get any weirder than mystics. They appear among us and seem to have little use for the way most people see the world. It isn't that they are always antagonistic to the lesser motivations of their fellow people—mystics often have deep compassion for the struggles of humans being human—it's just that they soar up to higher vantage points and see things about life, the universe, and everything that boggle our minds.

Mystics have a simplicity about their vision that is almost too pure for this world. What they have to say is usually so straight to the heart of things that our minds have a hard time finding handles on it. This is exactly how their messages need to be delivered.

Jesus told parables about birds and lilies and grains of wheat. He sat on a hilltop and gently laid out his vision for a different kind of world.

"Blessed are the poor in spirit: for theirs is the kingdom of heaven.
Blessed are they that mourn: for they shall be comforted.
Blessed are the meek: for they shall inherit the earth.
Blessed are they which do hunger and thirst after righteousness: for they shall be filled.
Blessed are the merciful: for they shall obtain mercy.
Blessed are the pure in heart: for they shall see God.
Blessed are the peacemakers: for they shall be called
the children of God...."

He went on to tell his followers,

"Ye are the salt of the earth... ye are the light of the world."

He was talking to men and women who were exhausted and bruised by life. His audience was filled with people who had been abused by oppressive rulers for many generations. He was telling them that not only was the kingdom of heaven within them, but also that they would gain it in the most paradoxical ways. Humility, meekness, mercy, purity, and peacemaking were to be the currency of the new powerful rather than swords and shields. It made no sense, but he said it anyway.

After many years of being raised in a fundamentalist Christian cult, I left the church and turned away from all things Bible. I learned how it had been stitched together, curated, twisted, and fabricated to serve the purposes of various powerful groups down through time. In my first book, there is a scene in which the main character's Bible was burned by his guides so that he could experience life without the rigid framework of beliefs he had been taught since birth. Later in the story, he encountered another guide who told him this:

"Your particular sect is an extreme case, but most who call themselves Christians hold a similar view—that their truth is the only truth. You are being called to see beyond one form and appreciate the vital Truth that flows through all. One day you will return to the dead ashes of your old Bible and discover new meaning. It will become an entirely different book for you. For now, trust that your journey afield will not leave you lost and abandoned."

I began to understand that, whoever this Jesus person was, when he referred to God or the "kingdom of heaven," he did not mean the same thing about them that traditional religion would have us believe. He was expressing a mystical way of experiencing the Big Everything.

We should not be surprised that they killed him for it.

The world has been misunderstanding and abusing mystics since day one for their audacity to suggest that things are much more than they appear to be.

Lao Tzu is said to have written the *Tao Te Ching*. Like Jesus, exactly who he was—or even if one man by that name really existed— is shrouded in the mists of history. I love one of the legends about how the strange and powerful words of the *Tao* came to be written.

Lao Tzu grew weary of watching the moral decay of society in Chengzhou and became certain that the kingdom was falling into decline. He escaped west on a water buffalo to live as a hermit in the great, unsettled desert frontier at the age of one hundred sixty. At the far border of the kingdom, a guard who was also secretly a disciple of his teachings recognized him. The sentry held him for several days and demanded that he write the teachings of the *Tao* for the good of the world before he would be permitted to continue on his journey.

Lao Tzu reluctantly agreed and what he wrote was said to be the *Tao Te Ching* with its eighty-one passages.

The first section of the *Tao Te Ching* reads—

The tao that can be told
is not the eternal Tao
The name that can be named
is not the eternal Name.
The unnamable is the eternally real.
Naming is the origin
of all particular things.
Free from desire, you realize the mystery.
Caught in desire, you see only the manifestations.
Yet mystery and manifestations
arise from the same source.
This source is called darkness.
Darkness within darkness.
The gateway to all understanding.

Lao Tzu and the other mystics express truths that rattle our reality tunnels. They walk a lonely path because most humans are invested in seeing through a fixed belief window. Mystics help us understand that there is a lot more to the whole picture. Even though we might not understand their paradoxes and metaphors, something in us thrills to know that we are connected to an intelligent system so imponderably massive that our minds cannot comprehend the wholeness of it for more than split seconds at a time.

Meister Eckhart wrote, *"If the only prayer you said in your whole life was, 'thank you,' that would suffice."* In this simple, potent sentence, he strips layers of sacred paint off the idea of prayer. What if we forget everything we know about prayer and just turn life into one continuous thank you? "Thank you for everything. Thank you for this next breath. Thank you for the ability to be here as myself for the tiny moment known as my life." His statement isn't complex, but it is mind-bending and life changing. That's what mystics do.

Human potential researcher Abraham Maslow talks a lot about the "unitive experience" in which a person suddenly breaks into a feeling that everything is somehow One Thing. He said, "*The great lesson from the true mystics, from the Zen monks, and now also from the Humanistic and Transpersonal psychologists, is that the sacred is in the ordinary, that it is to be found in one's daily life...in one's own backyard.*"

He also wrote, "*Self-actualizing people have a deep feeling of identification, sympathy, and affection for human beings in general. They feel kinship and connection, as if all people were members of a single family.*"

I read his book, *The Farther Reaches of Human Nature*, when I was struggling to find my place after several years of mystical breakthrough (and, truth be told, simultaneous nervous breakdown) during which I was not sure that I would ever be able to navigate the normal world again. He helped me understand that I was not alone and also that people who have these peak experiences eventually need to come down from the mountain top and walk among their fellow humans. Otherwise, what they have experienced is wasted because it is isolated and so lofty that it cannot be used in real life.

He pulled me out of the clouds with this thought:

"*The person in peak experiences feels himself, more than other times, to be the responsible, active, creating center of his activities and of his perceptions. He feels more like a prime-mover, more self-determined (rather than caused, determined, helpless, dependent, passive, weak, bossed). He feels himself to be his own boss, fully responsible, fully volitional, with more 'free-will' than at other times, master of his fate, an agent.*"

51

In other words, a mystical episode becomes practical when it activates this tremendous sense of personal power and a responsibility to live deeply.

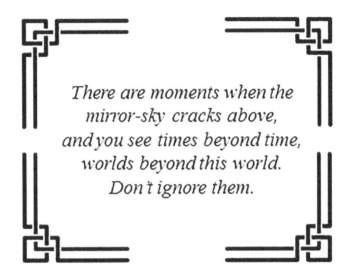

There are moments when the mirror-sky cracks above, and you see times beyond time, worlds beyond this world. Don't ignore them.

The reason any of this matters to us now is because we are called upon by the age in which we live to self-actualize. We have never reached such a peak of potential as a race before and, if we are going to do anything with it, we must step into the power of ourselves that lies beyond the common way of humans. Our era is begging us to do it.

Modern mystic Thomas Hübl said it well. "Responsibility is not a duty. Responsibility is my ability to respond authentically to the world."

To put this in immediate terms, you matter. I matter. Our own mystical experiences and epiphanies matter too. The moments of what C.S. Lewis called "flashes of pure northernness" that reveal our unbreakable connection to All That Is often come out of thin air. It is easy to ignore them with the rational thought of "…well, that was weird," but, when the mirror-sky cracks above us and we see times beyond time, for just a moment, we have experienced the mystical and ourselves as mystics. Most of us will never make the mystical life our full time occupation. That job seems to be reserved for just a few in the world. But we can take our place alongside those visionaries who have gone before with no sense of unworthiness because this anomalous way of seeing is part of our design. It is our long-forgotten birthright.

Most painters, writers, poets, troubadours, misfits, and heretics are mystics to some degree. The act of creation is mystical and we often cannot explain exactly how inspiration comes to us. Scientists like Albert Einstein, Nicola Tesla, and Buckminster Fuller spoke of what led to their discoveries with humility and awe. Mozart was a degenerate fool in most areas of his life, but when he sat down to write music, he tapped something transcendent. When we reach beyond the realm of common reason, we connect with the vast energetic matrix of information. When we bring some of it back to share with the world, we are doing the work of mystics because we are accessing the same Source.

G.K. Chesterson said it in *Orthodoxy*:

"Mysticism keeps men sane. As long as you have mystery, you have health; when you destroy mystery, you create morbidity. The ordinary man has always been sane because the ordinary man has always been a mystic. He has permitted the twilight. He has always had one foot in earth and the other in fairyland. He has always left himself free to doubt his gods; but (unlike the agnostic of today) free also to believe in them. He has always cared more for truth than for consistency. If he saw two truths that seemed to contradict each other, he would take the two truths and the contradiction along with them. His spiritual sight is stereoscopic, like his physical sight: he sees two different pictures at once and yet sees all the better for that. Thus he has always believed that there was such a thing as fate, but such a thing as free will also."

Mystics have always asked us to see the world through different eyes. They call us forward on the journey of meaning and purpose and destiny. They invite us to carry our own visions of what might be back to our lives and assist in the forward progress of evolution.

My friend Teresa "TJ" Phillips is a quiet, gentle spirit. As a young child, she had a prelude to the eternal self while gazing up at the stars. She saw herself and the whole world through eternal eyes. Her life was never the same after that. An NDE (what she calls a beyond-this-life experience) in her twenties, shifted her perspective of this awareness from the body self to an effortless understanding of the All and Nothing, and it became her natural state of being.

She has lived an essentially normal life of unconditional love and compassion for all, but has faced feeling like an outsider and being misunderstood while growing up; then difficult marriages, financial challenges, and poor health through what she calls the unfocused years. Through all of it, she carried the unshakeable knowing about life on this planet, a sense of peace amidst the chaos, and an insatiable fascination with living. It wasn't until recent years, after meeting people like me, that she understood how differently she sees this existence. She has a profound wisdom and has been instrumental in helping many people touch what is real and true in themselves. She came alongside me years ago and we have spent hours on the phone at times. There was something in her presence that helped me to become clear about my gifts. Sometimes during a long distance chat, the sound of a passing train will overwhelm the usual stillness of her Midwestern home, and we will have to wait until it roars and rattles away into the night before resuming our conversation.

In recent years, she has grappled with death more than once. Twice, after surgery, she fell into a coma. Her body was frozen, but she was able to see and hear discussions about "end of life options". She came out of the coma, but despite her powerful awareness, this experience rattled her human self and left behind a trail of trauma that has required her to undergo therapy and reach out for support from family and friends in a way she never had before. When I talk with Teresa now, she has even more compassion for her fellow humans and how we all struggle to be here in this life.

Teresa is not a famous mystic, preferring to share insights through conversation, stories, poetry and social media as Believe in the Moment. I include Teresa in this book out of gratitude for how she touched my life—and still does. She struggles with the ugly, painful stuff of being human and she also shows up with reminders that life is good, that my spirit is on a beautiful journey here as me, and that all of this is worth it. "Blessed is he who can laugh at himself, for he will never cease to be amused" is her favorite saying and way of letting me know everything will be all right.

That's what mystics do.

CHAPTER SIX

The Heretics

"If we have no heretics, we must invent them,
for heresy is essential to health and growth."
-Yevgeny Zamyatin

Of all the groups on the *Blessed Are the Weird* team, heretics have been the most likely to get burned, hanged, stoned, or otherwise mangled. They are found in every walk of life and they have no fixed occupation. No one would list Heresy as one of their skills on a resume. Being a heretic usually doesn't pay off in stock options, company cars, or dental plans.

In a funny way, the thread of heresy is found woven through all of the other Weird People types, though. As The Dude from *The Big Lebowski* might put it, "…that rug really tied the fuckin' room together."

There is something about the bold, radical spirit of heresy that is the heartbeat and lifeblood of creativity.

Yevgeny Zamyatin, a Russian dissident who wrote the dystopian 1921 novel *We*, said, "True literature can only exist when it is created, not by diligent and reliable officials, but by madmen, hermits, heretics, dreamers, rebels, and skeptics."

I am less interested in the idea of "true literature" than in what it takes to create anything true—anything different from what has already been created. In that, I agree with Mr. Zamyatin. Bureaucrats are good at keeping the status quo in place but terrible at creative solutions. Heretics will always be a thorn in the side of bureaucrats because they are too passionate and too curious. Like insistent children, they are forever asking hard questions. Like our Misfits from an earlier chapter, most of them don't set out to be heretics at all. They just aren't satisfied with the answers they keep getting to their honest questions. If you said, "You're such a heretic," most of them would probably shrug and reply with something like, "I only care about getting things moving forward again and I don't care who doesn't like it."

Trying to be a heretic for its own sake is on par with someone loudly proclaiming how weird they are. It isn't about that at all. There is no membership to the Heretics Club—imagining the idea of a board meeting for such an impossible group just made me snicker. The people who are so passionate about an idea that contradicts the beliefs of their society, company, family, church, or any other organization that they can't help but say it, and never give up until something changes, aren't doing it to get validation. Like every other member of the Blessed Weird tribe, they do what they do because some truth is alive in them. It is insistent, relentless, and inevitable.

Heretics are the early champions of ideas whose time has come.

As George Bernard Shaw once said, "Many of the great truths were blasphemy first."

We most often think of heretics and heresy in religious terms, but have a look at the Oxford English dictionary for a broader understanding of their importance:

her·e·tic

'here,tik/

noun

- A person believing in or practicing religious heresy.

- A person holding an opinion at odds with what is generally accepted.

synonyms: dissenter, nonconformist, apostate, freethinker, iconoclast

antonyms: conformist, believer

My heart rate picks up a bit when I read that list of synonyms—dissenter, nonconformist, apostate, freethinker, iconoclast. I suppose that isn't surprising, given the way I was raised. My parents were 1960s hippies before I was born. My father was a serious, intellectual type—less excited about the epic party that was going on back then and more engaged in trying to find answers to the meaning of life. My mother was smack in the middle of Haight Ashbury during its glory days. She dropped acid, hitchhiked across the country, backpacked through Europe, and joined the radical fringe of Bolshevik thinkers. They both yearned for something true, though. Shortly after I was born, they converted to Christianity and became members of a fundamentalist group. The fun times for hippies were coming to an end, and what remained was largely a lot of disillusioned kids who had to face a world that hadn't embraced Peace, Love, and Harmony despite their hopes that it would if they did enough acid trips. My parents dealt with that sense of chaos and disappointment by joining a radical group on the other end of the spectrum. Our lives in this church were consumed by conformity. Everything we did, said, and thought was governed by a strict set of standards. This included how we dressed, what we read, the music we listened to, and just about everything else. We looked like people out of *Little House on the Prairie* books. I never watched television or a movie until after I was twenty-five.

What bothered me most, though, wasn't living such an odd lifestyle. It was the fact that I wasn't allowed to ask questions. I was a true believer but often had questions and mystical experiences that weren't safe in that church. Unlike a lot of my friends, who knew how to play the game and do whatever they wanted when no one was looking, I wanted to believe and I only cared to know whether or not what I believed was true. When I began to suspect it wasn't—couldn't be—and discovered that no one I knew was willing to answer my honest questions, I began to feel strangled by conformity. Pull one dangling thread in that belief-fabric and the whole damn thing unravels. It was terrifying to watch everything I held on to so tightly about life turn into ropes of sand in my hands, but I also discovered the fierce, liberating joy of heresy. I learned that anything that can't stand the test of doubt doesn't deserve to stand at all.

This is why I love heretics, rebels, and nonconformists so much. They secretly delighted me as a child because they exuded a sense of unselfconscious realness that I could only envy. Now I love them even more because I know what their freedom costs—everything.

You know that crazy heart of yours?
The one with lightning crackling and
moonlight shining through it.
The one you've been told not to
trust because it often
led you off the beaten path.
The one so many have misunderstood
your entire life.
Trust it. Feed it. Grow it.
It is your greatest treasure
and will point
the way to your highest destiny.
It is the voice of your soul.

It is easy to assume that heretics and free thinkers are reckless spirits. Some are, that is true. In my experience, though, most people who endure the slings and arrows to gain their liberty use a great deal of care about how they exercise it. They also have a surprising humility about them as they go about their apostate business. Heretics aren't all bluster and public drumbeating. Often as not, they are reluctant heroes who were pressed into duty by the call of their own private truth. If the path they are compelled to follow leads them into speaking this truth in a public way, they will do that—but usually not for reasons other than the fact that anything less would be stopping short of completing their own mission to live deeply and honestly.

There is a reason we fear heresy. If we listen, we can hear the screams of heretics who have been murdered and tortured down through the centuries. The terror of their plight is embedded somewhere in our DNA. Perhaps we have long-buried memories of experiencing these things in lifetimes past. Regardless of why this fear is in us, the fact remains that we don't want to suffer for going against what is commonly agreed to be true. Our rational minds know better—we know that we probably won't be killed or tortured for saying or believing something contrary these days—but the irrational dread lingers in our limbic systems, triggering fight-or-flight feelings when we consider standing up for our own truth.

Famous thinker and heretic Bertrand Russell explained it this way: *"Conventional people are roused to fury by departure from convention, largely because they regard such departure as a criticism of themselves."*

Those of us who feel a great need to live out some truth that leads us off the beaten path need to remember that we trigger the fear of being wrong in others as we do this. It is a flip side of the coin from our fears of being persecuted for contradicting the wisdom of the herd. Now we can see another ancient fear in play—being wrong. Being wrong used to mean a number of bad things: ostracism, banishment, injury, getting lost, and death. In primitive survival situations, getting it right was a life-or-death proposition. Early humans couldn't afford to be wrong. They lived on the razor's edge of existence all the time. Getting it wrong often meant getting dead very quickly at the hands of nature or other people.

We have the luxury of being wrong now because we have developed safety nets to catch us if our wrongness turns out to have any consequences in real life. In most cases, being wrong means almost nothing now; however, when we live in some way that opposes the common agreement, we trigger fear in those who are most invested in keeping status quo beliefs, ideas, practices, and attitudes intact. It makes no rational sense why they should get riled, but they do because our very ability to live outside the lines freaks them out. It's not supposed to work that way and it might mean that they are wrong. If they are wrong about one thing, then maybe they are wrong about everything—and that thought is too terrifying for most who follow conventional wisdom to consider.

Seth Godin, a remarkable author and champion of new ideas, wrote this in his book, *Tribes—We Need You to Lead Us*:

"So the challenge, as you contemplate your next opportunity to be boring or remarkable, is to answer these two questions: 'If I get criticized for this, will I suffer any measurable impact? Will I lose my job, get hit upside the head with a softball bat, or lose important friendships?' If the only side effect of the criticism is that you will feel bad about the criticism, then you have to compare that bad feeling with the benefits you'll get from actually doing something worth doing."

Most of us live in places where we won't get tortured for going against the grain. We can level plenty of well-deserved criticisms against America, but we can stand up and tell our truth here with little fear of physical harm. In fact, if what we say is new and strikes a chord in people's hearts, we are more likely to be called upon to lead a movement whether we like it or not. As Seth Godin points out, probably the worst thing that will happen to us is that we get criticized. Criticism isn't any fun, but it's not the same thing as getting hit upside the head with a softball bat.

Heretics find themselves in a new situation these days. We need them more than ever and now they are more likely to make a major impact during their own lifetimes than at any other point in human history. The challenge for most modern heretics is not so much about keeping their heads intact—the real problem they face is keeping their heads about them when the hungry masses pick up their message. The powers that be in these days don't often need to kill the messenger. They only need to buy them, then co-opt and dilute their message. The keen edge of many a heretic's sword is blunted with cash and popularity. There is certainly nothing wrong with money and we can use the power of media distribution to our advantage like never before, so long as we understand the risk of losing ourselves and the passionate truth that motivates us in the bowels of the machine.

We have been handed an opportunity that heretics of the past could have only dreamed about. Whether or not we use it is up to us.

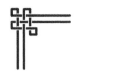

CHAPTER
SEVEN

The Painters

"I dream my painting and I paint my dream."
-- Vincent Van Gogh

Imagine this with me...

In times before we started keeping track of time, one of our ancestors picked up a handful of berries and smashed it into pulp. Then she smeared some of it on the cave wall and stood back to view this new thing she had done that had no name yet. In the flickering light of a small fire that burned nearby in its circle of rocks, the colors danced with shadows, illuminating her imagination. I wonder when she and primitive artists like her began to use powdered clays, animal blood, and other pigments to paint pictures depicting the drama of early life?

Like writers, artists who use paint to show us the world through their eyes are magicians. They are weavers who pull threads from their surroundings—and from within themselves—and use the looms of their imaginations to weave something greater than a mere copy of what they are using as a subject.

64

I am not particularly interested in art that is only representational—reproducing an image of something with almost photographic precision. I mean, the ability to do that is a magnificent talent, but I am most affected by art that meant something to the artist beyond the colors, lines, and shading of it. If a painting or drawing or photograph seduces me into a journey that leads inside the mind and emotions of the artist, I can be carried away by what compelled them too.

Like the others of our Blessed Weird gang, this one isn't exclusive to only those whose tools are paints and brushes. I use the word "painters" to represent those artists who offer us something beautiful, disturbing, rebellious, or revealing in a visual way. To put this in computer terms, if you click on the Painters icon, a whole file opens to reveal an array of photographers, painters, street artists, tattooists, sculptors and others.

Art is alchemy. The art that changes us has this power because it first changed the artist. When the artist sits down and begins the process of transmuting raw feelings, scraps of ideas, strands of fear, and visions of what might be into a picture, they are engaged in real magic. What comes out of that mage's fire is gold.

Ally Condie wrote in *Reached*,

"Writing, painting, singing—it cannot stop everything. Cannot halt death in its tracks. But perhaps it can make the pause between death's footsteps sound and look and feel beautiful, can make the space of waiting a place where you can linger without as much fear. For we are all walking each other to our deaths, and the journey there between footsteps makes up our lives."

I feel that it is all of that and more. All true art is an insurrection. Everything written, painted, or sung from the real, raw soul of us is a manifesto. Music that crackles through our hearts and bones is its own rebel yell. Anything less is unworthy of the warrior spirits alive within us.

Banksy is an English graffiti artist, political activist, film director, and painter. His satirical street art and subversive epigrams combine dark humor with graffiti. His works of political and social commentary have been featured on streets, walls, and bridges of cities throughout the world. He said this about art: *"Painting something that defies the law of the land is good. Painting something that defies the law of the land and the law of gravity at the same time is ideal."*

Like the Poets, some of the great artists who worked during oppressive times in history painted subversive codes into their works of art. They were often earning a living under commission by the rich and powerful, but found ways of telling their truths, which we are now unraveling.

We wait, starving for moments of high magic to inspire us, but life is a banquet of common enchantment waiting for our alchemists' eyes to notice.

Leonardo da Vinci painted a fresco on the church wall of Santa Maria delle Grazie near Milan. It is one of the most famous works of art in the world and the wall upon which it was painted was the only one left standing after Allied bombing during World War II demolished the rest of the building. We know this painting as *The Last Supper*. What most of us were never taught is that da Vinci, in his astonishing genius, revealed his own esoteric knowledge about the relationship between Jesus and Mary Magdalene and a lot of other heretical information using symbols to conceal other layers of meaning. His supposed conformity with the Church was a cloak that shielded him from torture and death during the vicious Inquisition. I can imagine him with a sardonic Madonna's smile on his face, painting scenes that the Church faithful would revere for centuries while he knew that some would understand his codes and keep their own rebellious faith during those days of peril and oppression.

I am no art scholar, but there are times when I stand before a painting and can feel the artist's soul in it. That is treasure and it is what this book is about—finding and revealing our souls. I love the artists who, whether I enjoy their style or not, manage to fight through the clouds of self-doubt and put their hands on that—something— that electric heartbeat that goes brushing, splattering, and bleeding onto the canvas. It is that something that helps us remember our own forgotten, hidden genius selves too. Or, as Jean-Luc Godard said, *"Art attracts us only by what it reveals of our most secret self."*

The painting on the cover of this book is an example of what I mean. How it came to me is one of those mysterious experiences of kismet. Years ago, I found an image floating around in the tides of social media. It was the figure of a person whose flesh and skin were cracked clay. This creature had an old wooden gate bolted across its chest, fastened with a rusty padlock. Brilliant light was shining from its heart through the slats of wood, seeking to burst out and illuminate everything around it. Without a single word, this painting told the story of awakening to the great, radiant treasure locked within.

Fast forward a few years as I was in the process of finishing this book. A picture scrolled down my screen and stopped my thumb. Here was another complete, eloquent tale told only with a paintbrush; an austere, rusting image with one sightless eye but the other round, wide, and seeping with green life. For me, it told the story of this book at a glance. Here we have a beautiful, functional (but lifeless and rusting) face of the world, but fresh, rebellious life with natural, ancient roots is growing behind that mask and can be seen only with a different eye. It wants to be seen. It wants to overflow and run down the rusting steel cheeks—the revitalizing tears of spring that can transform everything and make us remember the beauty and innocence of our natural selves.

I immediately began to search for the artist. Thanks to the sorcery of Google, I found him. The bio on his website reads: "Tomasz Alen Kopera, born in 1976 in Kożuchów, Poland. He attended the University of Technology in Wrocław, where he gained a degree in construction engineering. His artistic talent came to light already in early childhood. Tomasz paints in oil on canvas. Human nature and the mysteries of the Universe are his inspiration. His paintings permeate with symbols that often relate to human psyche and man's relation with the surrounding world. His paintings are dark and mysterious. The technique, developed over many years, testifies to the artist's great sensitivity and talent. Tomasz is celebrated for his acute attention to detail and mastery of colour. "In my work I try to reach to the subconscious. I want to keep the viewer's attention for a longer moment. Make him want to reflect, contemplate." In 2005, the artist moved to Northern Ireland where he lives now. From 2010, he has been a member of Libellule Group formed by Lukas Kandl."

I spent time strolling through his virtual studio. The paintings did that mysterious thing that is the thumbprint of true art—they made me feel. They made me remember ancient, disowned parts of me, possibly hints and scraps of memories from lifetimes past. They had that familiar, nameless quality that touches deep old wellsprings in hidden parts of my psyche.

I only hoped that he would be willing to grant me permission to use his art for the cover of this book. After several months of attempts, the stars aligned and Tomasz replied with a "yes." His story is important to me as further proof that real art is happening in our world and that it matters.

We need artists to keep showing us worlds through the eyes of their souls. They give us courage to keep going and keep trying— to keep chiseling away at our own statues of the Davids that wait, imprisoned within the blocks of marble until we liberate it and ourselves from the stone.

CHAPTER EIGHT

The Troubadours

My role in society, or any artist's or poet's role, is to try
and express what we all feel.
Not to tell people how to feel.
Not as a preacher, not as a leader, but as a reflection of us all.
— John Lennon

Every one of the *Blessed Weird* archetypes takes us back to something ancient and the Troubadours are no exception. These days, we have the king and queen makers of mass music distribution. Many modern singers and musicians are swallowed whole and spend their lives being digested in the alimentary tract of pop culture. I imagine quite a few of them started out with a troubadour's heart beating strong, but what has become of them after making deals with the devil is sad—not because they are earning millions of dollars, but because they have lost the raw, throbbing pulse of aliveness that first captivated us.

When I first wrote *Blessed Are the Weird*, I didn't know why the words came as they did. I remember "troubadours," though. It was the last of the list and it just had the right ring to it. There were connotations of flamboyance, romance, and unfettered joy in the flavor of the word. It conjured great castle halls, roaring fires, music and dancing, wine and wenches, long miles of road, and gypsy caravans. I had no idea at the time what a deep rabbit hole I had tumbled into by including this word.

Troubadours were a central part of the milieu in old Languedoc—a region of France that was a heartland for heretical and unorthodox ideas. If you follow history back to that time and place, you will find connections to the Cathars, Templars, and other holders of mysterious knowledge that the Church tried to stamp out as viciously as possible. Languedoc was ruled by the courts of Toulouse, and, during the eleventh and twelfth centuries, was the envy of Europe for its civilization and culture. The troubadours from this area were traveling minstrels whose love songs were essentially hymns to the Feminine Principle—the Goddess. Using ballads and love songs to disguise their true message, these wandering singers kept stories alive that would have gotten them burned at the stake had they come right out with what they were saying.

I don't mean to paint all of them as heroes. No doubt a lot of troubadours were simply singing for their suppers—as many do today. Quite a few were pawns in the hands of their rich patrons, singing what their masters wanted to hear. But there was a subversive movement of these musicians who had been trusted with dangerous truths and carried them far and wide through the Dark Ages in Europe. They sang of roses and ladies and romance. Hidden in their lyrics were threads of heresy hinting at sacred sexuality, grail quests, Rosicrucians, and mysteries that would threaten the growing power of an oppressive Church in that time.

The fact remains that we are touched by music in ways that we can't understand. It is a life-affirming element in our world and those who offer it to us from the depths of themselves are doing us all a great service. When I use the word "troubadour," I mean musicians and songwriters. They are people who sing the music of our hearts back to us and help us remember something or find what we have forgotten. They help us recover our souls.

I was driving into the mountains outside of Boise with my teenage twins a few days ago. We had just left cell phone coverage, so they were forced to put down their iPhones and look out the windows. I punched the power button on the car stereo and Bob Dylan started singing about Napoleon in rags and people with nothing to lose. After "Like a Rollin' Stone" ended, I talked with the kids about how Bob Dylan became the reluctant prophet-troubadour of his day. Megan, the most musically inclined of my children, lit up and told me how one of her school teachers made them listen to "The Times They Are a-Changin'" and "Blowin' in the Wind" as part of their class work.

"Meg," I said, "Bob Dylan tapped into the raw anger and confusion and longing for something real that so many people felt back then. He sang his songs and people loved him, even though he has a terrible singing voice. He helped them feel things out loud that they didn't know how to say. That's why I love him too."

Mos Def, actor, activist, and hip-hop troubadour, said it this way: *"Good art provides people with a vocabulary about things they can't articulate."*

Music that captures our hearts often has something rebellious and forbidden about it. It reminds us of what is free, wild, and divine in ourselves. It conjures pagan longings and animal pleasures and it also whispers the unsayable into the ears of our souls. It helps us feel our darkness and our light, our pain and our ecstasy. Troubadours who make this music help us ask questions about life and death and love—then they help us reach into the unknown for answers that we find in feelings rather than rational thought. They activate us in deep, hidden places and open our hearts to things we need and want to feel.

Isn't that why we so need to hear and make music? It reminds us of long ago times when we once danced and drummed and pounded our feet in the dust around a circle of campfire light. It transports us out of our mundane, isolated little worlds and plugs us back into the ancient heartbeat of the earth and all of its colorful people.

Sometimes we see musicians on stage, swept up in the raw intoxication of their own performance, push themselves to the line of madness and seem to step across it for a few moments. These are shamans who carry us with them on journeys into other worlds—into the garden of gods and goddesses and into scenes where mythical lovers find each other. We go there with them willingly because we know that we long for guides to help us as only they can. When they come back down to the stage and face the thunder of our screams and applause, sometimes we see barely hidden fear in their eyes because they know they have ventured beyond what is possible for humans to sustain.

And, like Icarus who flew too close to the sun, got his wings burnt, and fell down into the sea, sometimes these people can't keep it together. They are not normal and they become instruments of forces larger than themselves. It is not easy to be a servant of Hermes and the Muses and still maintain a human form. Many of them seem to shatter under the weight of their gift. Jim Morrison, Jimi Hendrix, Michael Jackson, Pink Floyd's Syd Barrett, Janis Joplin, Amy Winehouse, and many others simply couldn't handle walking this electric threshold. They left the stage in one way or another, but not before they showered us with brilliance.

It is this very thing they do—playing with fire and madness—that revives the parts of us that will never fit into the solemn world we have created. They pull us out of our seats, make us forget our own rules and dance, and help us soar into imagination like children again.

I have talked about my upbringing a bit so far, but I find it particularly interesting that groups like the ones I was raised in are scared shitless by the troubadours. I can't count the times I heard preachers tell us that rock music would lead us into unspeakable sins. They said things like, "…those drums make your body move and get you out of control." Yes, out of control. Isn't that a choice phrase? I am convinced that they were worried that music would lead to dancing and wanting to take our clothes off, and then probably right over the edge of the abyss called s-e-x. As I look at all of this in the rearview mirror, I know religious groups are not the only ones threatened by troubadours. Like comedians and other dissident members of our tribe, troubadours step forward and ask bold questions under the guise of their music. Since they aren't waving guns in the air, the control freaks and bureaucrats have a harder time pinning them down with charges of sedition. This doesn't soften the blow musicians wield against the status quo, though. They get into the hearts and minds of the young—who are less invested in keeping things tame and predictable—and help them ask questions for which they haven't yet found the words. It helps them feel their rage at being lied to by the adult world. For the older children among us, it helps us remember important feelings we have buried under an avalanche of possessions, responsibilities, and a lifestyle that is strangely suffocating despite its luxury. Music can help us remember how to plot our own prison break long after it seems we might have lost our will to do anything but stand in line.

That's because music is dangerous to everything that lacks soul.

CHAPTER
NINE

For They Teach Us to See the World through Different Eyes

We just met several members in the Blessed Weird People cadre. It is possible that I didn't make myself clear enough about the fact that these archetypes are not the only ones who belong on the team. Someone adapted my original piece and included "artists, music makers, and outsiders." Someone else made a version that added "gypsies, makers of music, dreamers of dreams, wanderers, vagabonds, and children." This illustrates my point. The list of titles could go on and on.

In a minute, I'm going to talk about various attributes of Blessed Weird people, but the one thing that is common to anyone who lives under this tent is the last phrase:

"For they teach us to see the world through different eyes."

There is a quality to the vision and work and lives of these people. They have leaned forward just beyond the forward edge of the status quo. They have followed a path of knowledge to the place where it leaves the map—and then kept going.

When someone does this, they expand the range of human possibility for everyone, just as the first person to walk on the moon forever changed our belief about something that had always been impossible before.

Magellan did it when he sailed around the globe and proved that our planet isn't a cube floating in space. This guy didn't fall off the edge of the earth into an abyss and, upon his return, the world was never—could never—be seen the same way again.

Roger Bannister demolished the accepted fact that no human could run the mile in under four minutes. Previously, everyone agreed that this wasn't possible and that our bodies simply could not do it. He did do it and made us wonder all over again what might be possible with these marvelous bodies that we had been assuming wasn't.

Louis and Marie Pasteur were not satisfied with the prevailing scientific knowledge that said bad-smelling air and water created a miasma that fostered disease. They stepped off the map and pressed the boundaries of understanding forward massively with their discoveries of microorganisms.

George Stephenson and his son Robert built a steam locomotive that could exceed twenty miles per hour. They demonstrated this mind-blowing speed despite dire warnings from pretty much everyone in the know about such things that the human body could not withstand that much velocity and would disintegrate in the attempt. After they simply didn't cooperate by exploding their display of the new machine, things got a lot faster in general—and have never really slowed down since.

Albert Einstein, Nikola Tesla, and Buckminster Fuller were scientists, but merely going as far as anyone had explored to that point could not satisfy their curiosity. They had this problem of audacity and insatiableness and indifference about anyone else's opinion of how things must be. Because of this, they changed the world. They taught us to see it through different eyes.

Weird People do this and it mostly isn't because they are trying to teach anyone anything either. We have this obsessive kink that won't let us settle into the tidy, respectable agreements that everyone has made about things up to this point. We are "allergic to dogma" as Rob Brezsny, author of *Pronoia*, might say. We have this radical desire to follow our inner longings no matter where they lead us—and we have come to understand that they are going to nearly always take us places most people aren't comfortable going.

In fact, this is why Weird People have always been the ones who move humanity forward. We are the ones willing to go to the verge of the horizon, where the known world disappears into mystery and uncertainty, to lean out over the raw edge of our own fear, and then take another step.

That sounds all poetic and mystical and shit, but it is what everyone who creates anything real does in extremely practical ways. Every single important step forward for humankind has been taken first by someone bold enough to question everything.

This is what Elon Musk is doing right this very minute. If anyone has bold ideas, this guy does. He seems to have picked up Nicola Tesla's own mantle and donned it over the chest and shoulders of a financially savvy entrepreneur. Not only has he amassed a huge fortune by altering the way money changes hands around the globe, he has tackled some of the modern world's stickiest energy problems.

Musk says that the goals of his SolarCity, Tesla Motors, and SpaceX projects revolve around his vision to change the world and humanity. His goals include reducing global warming through sustainable energy production and consumption, and reducing the "risk of human extinction" by "making life multi-planetary" by setting up a human colony on Mars.

I'm not too worked up about whether or not we should try to live on other planets, or even if global warming is a serious problem (this kind of nonchalance is going to get me killed by the more earnest types, I'm sure). What I love about Musk is his raised middle finger to the status quo. He has stepped forward and made massive investments in practical ways to break with the stupidity of how the establishment keeps energy locked up and enslaves humanity.

In 2014, he committed capitalistic treason by announcing that Tesla Motors will allow its technology patents to be used by anyone in good faith in a bid to entice automobile manufacturers to speed up development of electric cars. In other words, Elon Musk is willing to be called crazy or stupid or wrong by the financial elite so long as he can keep advancing the edge of his vision for a better world. He is questioning everything. I'm not even saying that he is a saint. He was and is one of the world's most highly paid CEOs. Clearly, he isn't pretending that everything he does is charitable. Even that level of honesty is refreshing. He is doing good and he is doing well for himself. I hope that he inspires a whole lot more business heretics to follow in his footsteps.

Creativity is audacious, but not for audacity's sake. It is audacious because it matches the very nature of the always-expanding Universe that forever breaks out of anything that has been created or decided before.

When it comes to a push between going all the way with life or stifling the urge under garments of respectability, Weird People have always been disrespectful, disagreeable, and downright ferocious about doing their own thing.

The process is often messy, unpredictable, and chaotic. The outcome is eventually something marvelous for everyone.

The outcome is magic.

When it comes right down to it, that's what this whole book is about. Magic.

Think about that for a minute.

From the Merriam-Webster Dictionary:

MAG·IC
ʻmajik/
- a power that allows people (such as witches and wizards) to do impossible things by saying special words or performing special actions
- tricks that seem to be impossible and that are done by a performer to entertain people
- special power, influence, or skill

I couldn't track down who said it, but Unknown wrote, "Magic is essentially the higher understanding of nature."

And there you have it. People who put one foot beyond the horizon of what has been possible and force everyone else to notice that our limits might be self-imposed do it because at some level they understand nature better.

They aren't doing what is actually impossible. They are doing what has always been there to do, but we just didn't know it—just couldn't see it.

"...for they teach us to see the world through different eyes."

That's the thing the world is starving for right now all over again. We have made blinding leaps forward over the last three or four decades—I mean several lifetimes' worth of change. We have a sense that too much is possible. We aren't sure we can handle much more of what we have been doing. In an odd way, we need to re-see everything. That might include making conscious choices about how much speed and change we really want to allow in our lives. Sounds funny to say it, but one of the most radical, creative things we might need at the moment is to slow down … to discover the magic of simple things again.

Somerset Maugham said, "Magic is no more than the art of employing consciously invisible means to produce visible effects. Will, love, and imagination are magic powers that everyone possesses; and whoever knows how to develop them to their fullest extent is a magician."

So it has come to this. Slower might be faster. Up might be down. Inside might be out.

Seems impossible. It always has.

That's where the Weird People come in. You might be one of them. Let's find out.

CHAPTER TEN

You Might Be A Weird Person If...

You need to be a little bit crazy.
Crazy is the price you pay for having an imagination.
It's your superpower. Tapping into the dream.
It's a good thing, not a bad thing.
— Ruth Ozeki

We have been talking about all of these fascinating creative types as "them," but now it is time to turn and face each other for the remainder of this book. If you are willing to do that now, I want to sit down across from you, move in close enough so our knees touch, and meet your eyes with mine. Let's talk in terms of how this affects us—you and me—right here, today, in our real lives and what we can do about it.

The truth is, not everyone is weird. Not in the way we're talking about here. Sure, everyone has weird little quirks in their personality, but not everyone has lived through the difficult experience of not fitting in. Most have not taken the terrifying inward journey to discover what is awkwardly brilliant and beautifully cracked. I don't blame them either. Life as a weird person is hard—especially before we find our tribes and get comfortable in our strange skins. Most people, if they think about it at all, would rather just be normal. It is a lot easier.

After I originally shared *Blessed Are the Weird*, I became known as The Weird Guy. Then people began posting anything with the word "weird" to my Facebook page under the assumption that I would be overjoyed. I got pictures with goofy faces, bizarre tattoos, and all manner of sayings that suggested "Everyone's weird." People started sending me pictures of themselves with dyed hair and piercings, saying, "Hey, look! I'm a total weirdo. See?" It took me a long time to figure out why this annoyed me. I am an inclusive person and I want everyone to feel safe to crawl out of their shell, even if that process is awkward. Blessed Weirdians really are different from most other people. I know that everyone has depths to plumb, but not all of them have been forced by life to do it as we have. And doing it might mean some outward expression that makes us obvious, but those are usually just window dressing for insecurities.

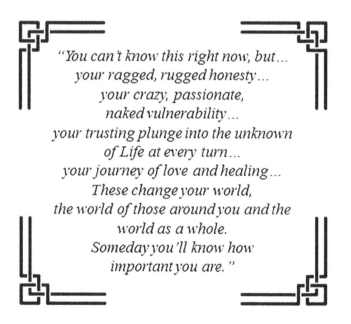

"You can't know this right now, but...
your ragged, rugged honesty...
your crazy, passionate,
naked vulnerability...
your trusting plunge into the unknown
of Life at every turn...
your journey of love and healing...
These change your world,
the world of those around you and the
world as a whole.
Someday you'll know how
important you are."

There is a distinction between merely weird and Blessed Weird. The Blessed Weird aren't that way to get attention. We have this quality of being scooped out by life; hollowed and chiseled, beaten and refined. Blessed Weirdians are exhausted by anything that isn't real. Most of us find dogma or prevailing opinions toxic. We aren't likely to jump on bandwagons or join popular crusades. We are skeptical about magic bullets, one-minute fixes, or tidy seven-step solutions to anything. We have been living this life as ourselves the hard way for a long time. We know better than to imagine that merely reading the right books or sharing intelligent memes or getting tattoos or dressing like <insert popular nonconformist idol here> will satisfy our need to do life our way—all the way.

If you are reading this book, you have probably lived your whole life with the painful gift of not fitting in. I don't mean that you can't handle yourself in social situations or keep a job. Many of us appear completely normal to the outside world and it is only in our private selves that we know the truth.

One of the forces that drove me to write this book—and certainly the reason I'm writing this chapter now—is to let you know that you are not alone. Quite the opposite is true. You may not fit in with normal society and you may not even fit in with the various groups of supposedly rugged nonconformists, but you are part of a long lineage of people who were once honored for their gifts and strange abilities. Though we were scattered and had to hide our lights, now we are finding each other.

Here are a few attributes of Blessed Weirdness you may recognize in yourself. As we explore these together, notice which ones describe you, but please realize that I don't pretend that this is a comprehensive list. The only reason I describe these characteristics at all is to offer a starting place for you to recognize those things about yourself you may have always assumed were broken but may very well become your greatest strengths—and offer clues about your own unique purpose and destiny.

You might be a Blessed Weird Person if…

Personal comfort is not your highest priority. We are much more concerned with living out our own strange and insatiable truth than with making sure our boat doesn't get rocked.

You feel that you have lived several lifetimes already in this current one. It surprised me to discover that many people have a relatively stable trajectory through life in terms of the way they view the world and themselves. Most weird people tell me that their entire lives have changed so radically that they can barely remember being the person they once were. Robert Anton Wilson, in his book *Prometheus Rising*, talked a lot about "reality tunnels"—the psychological structure through which our minds perceive the world. This includes how we see ourselves, how we interact with society, what we believe about right and wrong, and how we feel as we navigate the whole thing. Many people are able to maintain what might be called a normal reality tunnel that grows larger as they mature but never gets dramatically shaken up. This means they are probably comfortable with the beliefs and attitudes of their accustomed tribes at work, church, home, and social settings. They become skillful at the vernacular, appearance, and modes of relating in those circles. This gives them a strong sense of comfort and certainty. Many, if not most of them, never feel the need to examine themselves deeply because of this comfort level. Why fix what's not broken? Weird people have often lived through major disruptions that force us to adjust to entirely different ways of seeing the world—and being in it too. This might include divorcing parents, abuse, death of important family or authority figures, extreme religious upbringing, frequent household moves, poverty, and other factors. The disruption may be internal and caused by sexual orientation issues (especially if this is frowned upon by the family or social group in which we were raised), psychological deviations from "the norm," physical abnormalities, or unusual emotional sensitivities. However or why-ever it happens, we have experienced tremendous personal changes that make it impossible to believe that the world is only one way. We have already lived through more change in one lifetime than many people might experience in two or three. Because of this, we have a strange and potentially wonderful way of seeing what most people can't. Their brains filter these things out as unimportant or irrelevant, whereas ours notice them.

You have sensitivities or perceptions that set you apart. We might add to our list of Blessed Weirdians with psychics, visionaries, empaths, shamans, healers, witches, seers, clairs, and others. As I explained earlier, the initial group that appeared in *Blessed Are the Weird* was peopled with several placeholders who represent the whole troupe. I don't mean that all weird people talk to dead people or can heal with their hands, but I do mean that many of us have native gifts that didn't fit well in society or perhaps even the family in which we were raised. This means we probably hid these things from others—and often denied ourselves access to them as well. Waking up to Who We Really Are is such a relief because we can finally pay attention to and develop these abilities that have remained quietly urgent inside for so long. You may not know why you can walk into a room and read the energy—sometimes you just know you have to leave, even if that creates an awkward situation. You may be keenly intuitive but have never known how to use the strange knowings that come over you at times. These perceptions and sensitivities are gifts, but they often make us feel crazy in a world where so few others seem to share them with us, or would be able to understand if we tried to explain. I suspect that Harry Potter became wildly popular partly because we have a lot of people in the world who wish they could attend Hogwarts rather than the Muggle schools. Harry, Ron, and Hermione make us imagine ourselves as their classmates and we know we would fit right in—even if our particular twist of magic doesn't fall into the strict category of wizardry. In my own life, for example, I often had ecstatic, mystical experiences of beauty that I had no way of expressing to those around me. I tried, but then I would get strange looks from my friends and the process of partial shunning would begin. The thing is, though, denying our sensitivities and gifts makes us sick. We might develop psychoses, depression, or physical problems because we have suppressed the impulses of our own souls. We might have a nervous breakdown that can't be explained by anything other than the fact that we have ignored what's real for too long. Learning to accept and use our anomalous gifts is a prescription for health.

You want to live differently from the world around you. Weird people often know how to carry on their lives in usual-looking neighborhoods, go to normal jobs, and drive cars that don't stand out of the crowd. What this doesn't mean is that we feel at all comfortable with the rat race. Our basic attitude about life is different. We don't operate under the common assumptions about almost anything. If we learn to play the game, we frequently feel distress about the rules and how the players are expected to treat each other. Not all weird people are environmentalists, but most of us have an uneasy sense that living high-consumption lifestyles is a bad idea—even if we aren't sure exactly why. It's just something we know. We don't fall into the template that says that the greatest value in life is gained by making piles of cash. That's not to suggest that we must take a vow of poverty. Many weird people are rich, but we seem to place more priority on expanding our souls in delight with what we do for a living than on racing up the corporate ladder. In other words, we define happiness differently.

You are passionate. Weird people usually struggle with balance. Most of us have probably been told some version of "man…you are intense sometimes." We don't always know the right codes to be cool. We are lovers of life. We go all in. We are vulnerable. We laugh a little too long and loudly. We are tremendously serious about things that matter to us. We care. We have huge, open hearts—even though some keep them guarded because they have been wounded in the past. We seem to have little regard for personal pain if it means we are following our hearts, but we usually worry whether or not those around us will be okay while we are doing our thing. We tend to get insecure and obsessive at times in our attempts to right the ship and keep up with other people (or slow down for them). We become reclusive when our inner fire is depleted by too much activity that isn't aligned with our natures.

You have a sense of purpose. We might not know exactly what it is, but we have been on an unusually urgent quest to find it for as long as we can remember. This isn't to suggest that everyone doesn't want to find their purpose, but most are willing to accept some version of it as "good enough" if it gains them entry into the right job, plenty of money, and all the other common markers of success. We can't accept these answers. Many of us have tried, but it just didn't work— which left us feeling more confused and marooned than before. We watch the rest of the world rolling along just fine and we can't figure out what is wrong with us that we can't be happy with the shiny veneer. There's nothing wrong with us. We show up with the need to answer the questions our own way, and, because we are asking bigger questions, we require more magnificent answers.

This list could get a lot longer, but I am confident you can see the pattern. If you noticed yourself saying, "Yes…that's me" a few times, you are almost certainly one of the Blessed Weird people to whom I am writing. Welcome to humanity's dream team. The world needs us to know who we are. It also needs us to do our thing like never before.

Andréa Balt, founder of Rebelle Society and Creative Rehab, wrote, *"Your weirdness will make you stronger, your dark side will keep you whole, your vulnerability will connect you to the suffering of our world, your creativity will set you free. There is nothing wrong with you.*"

I don't like exclusive clubs and that's not what I'm trying to set up here. We didn't show up in this time and place to look down on the normal world—even though it has been disregarding us for many, many years. This isn't about taking revenge or helping karma right a lot of wrongs. That does nothing but activate what Transactional Analysis founder Stephen Karpman called "The Drama Triangle" in which the Victim becomes the Persecutor who is then confronted by the Rescuer—and the cycle continues.

No, this is about stepping out of that ages-old wheel of pain and simply being who we are in truth and beauty. That is what the world desperately needs, even if it does not know how to ask for it nicely yet. You and I, with all our cracks and quirks, are called forward to form a vanguard of something new.

I found this quote and it describes the journey of excruciatingly sensitive and self-conscious people:

"Empathetic people – dreamers and idealists – have this sort of accidental power. Most spend their early years ridden with self-doubt, insecurity, and people pleasing habits. But their journey is inevitably derailed when this comfortable life gets uprooted by an unexpected darkness. Suddenly their trusted methods no longer seem to bring them happiness. At first this depression convinces them that they might never feel joyful again. But ultimately, it sets them on a quest for something more – for love, justice, and wisdom. Once this adventure begins, there is no stopping a dreamer. And when dreamers unite? Well, that's how we start to change the world." – Unknown

In general, Weird People are highly self-conscious. We tend to observe the world—and ourselves—constantly in ways that other people don't. We watch our own mind and watch our mind watching itself! This makes for a lot of awkwardness. We feel things more deeply. We notice things. We are curious and interested in the quirky details that most people find meaningless. We are willing to be wide-broken-open over and over again. In fact, even though it means walking around with our nerve endings exposed, we wouldn't have it any other way.

Your superpower is your sensitivity. Your sensitivity is also your Achilles' heel. Your greatest gift to the world is on the flip side of the same coin as your greatest wound. In fact, if you aren't sure what your gift is yet, take a look at what always brings you down—take a look at your darkest, weakest stuff. That will give you clues. On the reverse side of your deepest shadow, you will find your brightest light.

Most Weird People I know are only truly afraid when they start to get numb. Our depth of feeling—our ability to sense things and constantly process them—is our most valuable currency in this world, even if it isn't always easy to turn it into cash in the bank. But somehow, we know that if we stamp, stuff, or dampen all of these often-uncomfortable sensations, we will have lost what makes us real.

And that is probably the most important attribute of all—an abnormal desire for what is real. We can't abide a life that is not real. It might be hard to figure out. It might take us a long time to carve out our own niche. But every Weird Person I have ever met has a backbone of iron hidden under their layers of self-consciousness and sensitivity. Even the most gentle among us are determined to keep going, keep fighting, keep chiseling away until we are satisfied with the shape of our own lives.

Perhaps the most powerful and concise way to find out if you are among the Blessed Weird is if your heart leaps up and say, "Yes!" to the following passage:

"The truly creative mind in any field is no more than this: A human creature born abnormally, inhumanly sensitive. To him... a touch is a

blow, a sound is a noise, a misfortune is a tragedy, a joy is an ecstasy, a friend is a lover, a lover is a god, and failure is death. Add to this cruelly delicate organism the overpowering necessity to create, create, create – so that without the creating of music or poetry or books or buildings or something of meaning, his very breath is cut off from him. He must create, must pour out creation. By some strange, unknown, inward urgency he is not really alive unless he is creating."

    - Pearl S. Buck

CHAPTER ELEVEN

This Is Personal

"An artist is someone who uses bravery, insight, creativity, and boldness to challenge the status quo. And an artist takes it personally."
– Seth Godin

In the first chapter, I said that we are living in a time of great crisis. Even though the planet is swarming with more people than ever before and awash in ideas, what we are going through isn't about anyone else. It is about you and me. You are the only one living your life. I'm the only one living mine. For the moment, there are only the two of us here having this moment of truth.

We live in a time during which it is so easy to float along on eddies of comfort. Very few of us are anywhere near the bare wire of survival—ever. We have developed so many ways to survive, so many safety nets, that we rarely have to actually face ourselves and ask deeper questions about what we really want. It is too easy to get up every morning, find the familiar ant trails to work, follow them all day long, come home to our nests at night, and numb out in front of the television or computer with a big plate of food. There is nothing wrong with routines, entertainment, or food, of course.

The problem is the numbing.

The problem is that we have forgotten how to make our own lives works of art and we cannot seem to find enough ways to gorge ourselves to fill the aching sense of emptiness this leaves behind. Because we don't know how to fill up the space of our lives with ourselves, we turn that job over to others and then wonder why we are never satisfied.

Our young men and women face futures that appear both uncertain and uninspiring to them because we haven't answered the question and they don't trust us to guide them with our words or our examples. Most of us weren't offered initiation into adulthood and we haven't given them the necessary rituals of passage so that they know that they must take their places as responsible members of the tribe. As a result, they go to college hoping to figure something out along the way that feels right.

A number of years ago, I worked for a government agency in Austin, Texas and sometimes managed part-time helpers who were the teenage sons of bureaucrats higher in the food chain. They wanted their kids to have summer work, so these boys would come help me in the warehouse. We stacked boxes and stuck labels, and I would ask them about their college plans. I was disturbed by how lost and terrified they all seemed about their lives. None of them had any real idea what they wanted to do or even why they were going to college. I was going through a time of deep transformation and self-discovery, and wasn't in much better shape than they were in that regard, but I was particularly interested in solving the puzzle of purpose.

I asked one of them, "Well, what does your dad do for a living?"

He said, "Oh, you know, he's a manager or something."

"So, what does he actually do, though?"

He stopped in mid-lift and froze with a box teetering on the edge of a shelf. "Um, I really don't know. I think he goes to meetings and checks emails—things like that."

He had no idea what his father did to provide the upper middle class lifestyle he had been raised to expect. His father had not offered him anything but the veneer of comfort. As we talked, it became clear that this young man didn't want to spend the next forty years in a cubicle, but he didn't know of any alternatives. He didn't know how to find himself or what he wanted to do.

He had no sense of his own mission or purpose in life. What troubled me even more, though, was that he didn't seem to have any passion to find it for himself and was just climbing onto the conveyor belt with a shaky assumption that it would carry him somewhere good. His eyes met mine a few times during this conversation and the fear in them was painful for me to witness.

That was no isolated instance either. I had many such conversations and began to detect an invisible epidemic that has spread throughout the developed world. We don't know what our purpose for living is and we are terrified to admit it to anyone—especially ourselves. Instead, we run faster, take on more debt, work harder, and hope that the Purpose Fairy will sneak up and hand us a magic scroll with our life's mission written on it. We are desperate to feel that our lives matter and we have a terrible suspicion that they might not.

It is no wonder that first world countries have the highest levels of clinical depression on earth. When humans live close to the survival line, the main question they have to answer about their purpose every day is "Can I find enough food to live another day?" If they do, they have fulfilled their mission and can relax. In many primitive places around the world, when the needs of basic survival are met, people spend a lot of time connecting with each other around the village fire. They sing, dance, and make music. They don't have much opportunity to better their material lives, but they have a sense of richness in their human experience that we in richer countries would envy if we took time out from our mad pace to notice the critical things we are missing. This is a strange time on earth, especially in

America. Surrounded by so much luxury, almost no one knows how to luxuriate. Instead, we kill ourselves about the business of getting more luxury. That's like starving to death at a banquet.

I don't believe that the answer to our modern question of purpose will be found in trying to turn the clock back to primitive days. Some have made this choice and it can work, but that requires radical dedication to a lifestyle that most of us don't really want. Let's face it, we love toilets that flush, smooth roads, and the lunch buffet at Whole Foods. As a species, we worked hard to get here.

We have solved many of the survival problems that once made our lives "poor, nasty, brutish, and short," to borrow and twist a phrase from Thomas Hobbes. What we haven't solved is the puzzle of purpose.

I am convinced that the great mission of our day is not conquering the sea or space, disease, or tyranny. We haven't quite figured all of those things out yet, of course, but the grand quest that calls to the hero in every one of us is to become fully alive. Becoming fully alive means that we must stand up, shake ourselves from the inertia of numb lifestyles, and learn what it means to be dynamic creators—then do something about it. In a funny paradox, many of us may find our great mission in one of those tasks—conquering disease and tyranny, exploring the outer reaches of space, or some other external quest—but not before we have discovered our inner why. It is no longer an either-or proposition; it's both. We have bumped our heads against a ceiling on Maslow's hierarchy of human needs. We can't be satisfied until we break through it into a new experience of self-actualization.

Sounds exhausting, doesn't it?

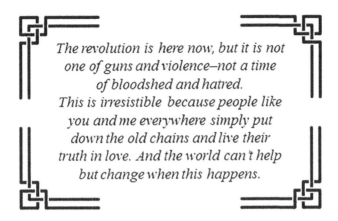

The revolution is here now, but it is not one of guns and violence—not a time of bloodshed and hatred. This is irresistible because people like you and me everywhere simply put down the old chains and live their truth in love. And the world can't help but change when this happens.

What I'm really talking about is becoming indispensable to ourselves. If we have a tremendous sense that our whole lives are these works of art that we are busy creating every day, we know for sure that no one else can replace us. We aren't like the others and we don't want to be. That's when life becomes personal. That's when it becomes art whether or not we know how to make music, paint, or write.

Seth Godin says it beautifully in his book, *Linchpin: Are You Indispensable?*

Art isn't only a painting. Art is anything that's creative, passionate, and personal. And great art resonates with the viewer, not only with the creator.

What makes someone an artist? I don't think it has anything to do with a paintbrush. There are painters who follow the numbers, or paint billboards, or work in a small village in China, painting reproductions. These folks, while swell people, aren't artists. On the other hand, Charlie Chaplin was an artist, beyond a doubt. So is Jonathan Ive, who designed the iPod. You can be an artist who works with oil paints or marble, sure. But there are artists who work with numbers, business models, and customer conversations. Art is about intent and communication, not substances.

An artist is someone who uses bravery, insight, creativity, and boldness to challenge the status quo. And an artist takes it personally.

That's why Bob Dylan is an artist, but an anonymous corporate hack who dreams up Pop 40 hits on the other side of the glass is merely a marketer. That's why Tony Hsieh, founder of Zappos, is an artist, while a boiler room of telemarketers is simply a scam.

Tom Peters, corporate gadfly and writer, is an artist, even though his readers are businesspeople. He's an artist because he takes a stand, he takes the work personally, and he doesn't care if someone disagrees. His art is part of him, and he feels compelled to share it with you because it's important, not because he expects you to pay him for it.

Art is a personal gift that changes the recipient. The medium doesn't matter. The intent does.

Art is a personal act of courage, something one human does that creates change in another.

When we understand that our unique selves and the lives we live are meant to be art, all of us can accept this dare to challenge the status quo. What I mean by status quo is the soul-deadening homogeny that stands there like a great, stupid thug blocking us from passing through the gate into a life that is satisfying because it is our own.

I suspect that is why you are reading *Blessed Are the Weird People* right now. You don't want to fit into someone else's mold until the day you die. In fact, you probably haven't been fitting in very well your whole life. Now it's time to do something with this complex, sometimes-awkward gift of who you are.

CHAPTER
TWELVE

It's Not Optional

"We're not on our journey to save the world but to save ourselves.
But in doing that you save the world.
The influence of a vital person vitalizes."
— Joseph Campbell

One of the challenges we face is a tendency to believe that someone else will get the job done. We stifle our native powers of creativity in favor of letting the geniuses handle things. We vote for them, buy their books, watch their movies, give to their causes, and get in line behind them because it is easier to believe that they know something we don't. They are much richer, more powerful and influential, so we should just do what they say. Plus, they seem to have formidable focus, drive, and work ethic and their accomplishments intimidate us because we aren't sure we have the necessary skill and stamina to get the job done.

It is not because we are lazy—although sometimes we are; let's be honest here—we just have not given our own genius its proper value. Because this is true, we find a million reasons to procrastinate rather than begin the process of excavating our inner gold.

Being creative is not a luxury reserved for people with some special artist gene. Tapping our inherent genius is critical to our survival and evolution--now more than ever before. It really means that we are willing to live the full, dynamic life that is coded right into our blood and bones. It means that we turn all of life into a thriving dance whose steps and music we make up as we go. But make no mistake …

It isn't optional.

To live uncreatively is to give up on life itself and accept the lie that all the best stuff has already happened in this world or in our own lives. It is a slow suicide of purpose.

Mary Oliver said, *"The most regretful people on earth are those who felt the call to creative work, who felt their own creative power restive and uprising, and gave to it neither power nor time."*

In the gnostic *Gospel of Thomas,* it is written, *"If you bring forth what is within you, what you bring forth will save you. If you do not bring forth what is within you, what you do not bring forth will destroy you."*

Mia Hollow says, *"Every now and again, you will feel a dull ache in your soul. A gentle humming around your heart. A longing for something without a name. If I ever told you to obey anything, this would be it. Listen to the call of your authentic self; that part of you that lives just outside of your own skin. Let it have its way with you. I have died a hundred times trying to ignore it."*

And Abraham Maslow wrote, *"A musician must make music, an artist must paint, a poet must write if he is to be ultimately at peace with himself. What one can be, one must be."*

I am more concerned with that last phrase, "…what one can be, one must be," than I am with whether or not you consider yourself a musician, artist, or poet, though. As we discussed in the last chapter, life is art. What comes from the deepest part of you is your art, whether that is math equations, poetry, feats of engineering, or raising amazing children. You can express your peculiar genius any way you must and it won't matter if it doesn't come out in some fashion that we would normally consider artistic.

But realizing our potential is not easy. If you are like me, you have many "uprisings of creative power," but then it is time to pick up the kids from school, make dinner, check email, squeeze in some exercise so we don't get any fatter, finally crawl into bed, and maybe watch an episode or six of *Orange Is the New Black* before falling asleep.

Part of the reason this is especially true these days is because of three things.

First thing, we actually have more potential than people before us did. The ceiling is higher. The sheer immensity of what is possible is often overwhelming. I will describe this situation in more detail shortly.

Second thing, we have far more distractions than ever before. Remember the days before the Internet exploded in our faces? I wonder what the hell we did with our time before Facebook, YouTube, Twitter, Tumbler, Pinterest, Instagram, Snapchat, and LinkedIn—not to mention Netflix and Amazon and the NFL Network (according to a 2014 Nielsen study, the average American household receives 189 cable channels, so... you get the picture). In a single generation, we have created a virtual layer to life that might have set us all free, but instead somehow seduces us into spending all our time and money in ways that keep us working harder than ever.

Third thing, and this is the big one, we live in a culture that values the worth of something by how popular it becomes, how much money it generates, or how famous its creator is. Often when we have the impulse to start chipping away at something important to us at a deep level, the first voice that shows up inside is one that says, "Yeah, but you won't make any money, so why bother? You'll never be able to quit your job doing that." I know many people who want to write a book, learn to play music, or start a community project, but, instead of pulling the dangling thread of their desire, they put in more time at the office because the reward is more tangible—money or its equivalent in career advancement.

How many frustrated artists do you know who won't make time to develop their amazing stuff because they can't see how it will ever turn into a full time income? Instead, most of us defer doing what is important to us now in hopes that we can bank enough cash to buy our freedom someday and do it later.

The Muses get impatient when we refuse to pay attention to their nudges. Inspiration to bring forth something magnificent dies over time when we fail to heed its call. Little by little, faster and faster, the years pass while we stay busy pouring our vital energy into maintaining lifestyles that lack the deep satisfaction we have always wanted. It is not that we can't make the time to follow our hearts. We can. We can use our power of "yes" and "no" to prioritize and cut. Our problem lies in not valuing our own inner treasure enough to do anything about it. We keep waiting to be crowned before taking our own throne. It doesn't work that way.

Being crowned is just the public acknowledgement of what has already happened behind the scenes as a result of millions of micro-choices in the direction of our dreams.

I can't promise you (or myself, for that matter) that working at the process of revealing our truest dreams will yield fame or piles of cash. As I said earlier, that idea is an obstacle by itself. If we can't lay aside the notion of getting any kind of guarantee that our work will turn into a full-time income, we will be stuck in the numb no-man's-land of mediocrity—never quite able to excavate our best stuff because we can't bear the risk that it might not pay off in ways that society values. Fuck society!

Hunter S. Thompson wrote a prescription for the antidote:

"As things stand now, I am going to be a writer. I'm not sure that I'm going to be a good one or even a self-supporting one, but until the dark thumb of fate presses me to the dust and says 'you are nothing,' I will be a writer."

I need to be startlingly clear.
This thing of finding
your authentic voice,
expressing your blessed weirdness
and revealing your soul
isn't an elegant process.
You don't do it to be cool.
You don't do it to get laid or get rich.
It's only real when it is ruthless,
relentless, and inevitable.
But it is also a matter of personal
and collective survival.
Yes, it's that important.
You are that critical.

I am typing these words at 3:33 a.m., lying on my belly in bed. I dozed off earlier but then woke up and couldn't get back to sleep— even though I went out to the kitchen and ate three large spoonfuls of refried beans out of the fridge, watched two *Game of Thrones* episodes, tried to astral travel for a while with the lights out, and meditated on imaginary names in the phone book. The trouble is, this manuscript is working me over night and day now. Just before I flipped the laptop open and started writing this paragraph, I almost tried to numb out with more episodes of something on Netflix. The choice was right there, floating in the dark patches beneath my eyelids as I decided whether to chip away at a few hundred more words or maybe see if I could use someone else's stories to put me under. It would have been easy to let these thoughts swirl around like a tornado of confetti in my mind, make plans to remember them in the morning, then click the play button on some show that would hopefully let me slide into an alpha brain wave state and maybe get tricked into sleeping for a few hours before it is time to get started on a new day's routine of work.

Right there. That's a micro-choice. I often don't make them in the direction of my own dreams, and when I don't, I get stuck and discouraged. My internal nudges and genius ideas fade into a miasmal of thoughts like "…I'm not sure if that would have worked anyway."

Crowning happens when we make enough of those tiny decisions to take actions that seem ridiculously insignificant at the time but later turn into a completed project through the process of relentless accrual. Michelangelo raises his mallet and chisel even though he wants to be hanging out in the forum with his friends, drinking wine and gossiping about what the Pope's mistress was wearing at the theater last night. *Chink… chink… chink…* About three years later, forty men push a wooden cart bearing the fourteen-foot-tall statue of *David* into the heart of Florence.

What adds another twist to this example is that Michelangelo started working on *David* with nothing but a gigantic block of marble that two other sculptors had abandoned because it had imperfections that they couldn't imagine their way around. They walked away from this chunk of raw potential and it lay there for more than twenty-five years before a brash young artist came along and agreed to make something of it.

In my work with writers, I often prescribe a regimen of one thousand words per day—but I'm happy if they write just five hundred and take weekends off. The math works out to twenty-five hundred words per week. Do this for a year with two full weeks off for vacation and they have drafted a whole book of over three hundred pages. That is an inexcusably easy pace. Five hundred words do not take that long to write. It's also the easiest thing in the world to find reasons not to do.

We can apply this thought process to anything from losing weight to starting a company. Whatever is in our hearts to do—and I'm talking about those things that are insatiable in us—can be approached from this one-snowflake-at-a-time mindset. No, we won't start an avalanche tomorrow at that rate but keep at it in spare scraps of time every day, and after a while, something cracks. The hillside starts to slide and everything goes into momentum.

The title of this chapter is *It's Not Optional*. I am convinced that we face a situation in our world that can only be solved by a whole lot of us realizing our creative potential. When I say "real"-ize, I mean "to make it real"—not just come to a mental realization of it. We cannot sit by and hope that the Creative Genius 1%-ers will figure everything out and hand us the answers we require. What needs to happen right now must begin right in the backyard of our own lives. There are too many of us on earth at the moment to let a tiny minority of inspired people carry all the weight. It's not fair, and, even more to the point, it won't work.

In older times, children of nobles and aristocrats were taught the principle of *noblesse oblige*. It is a French phrase that literally means "nobility obliges." The scions of wealth and power were told that being to the manor born brought with it the obligation to use the privileges of their position for noble purposes. In other words, they needed to perform acts of service for those less fortunate and step into leadership roles for which their money and education prepared them. We are all children of great wealth if we live in First World countries, and we have been handed immense opportunities along with our birth certificates.

We love to pretend that we have it hard, but we really don't. We live in fertile territory to do anything we desire—without asking anyone's permission. We have everything we need and it is only our own inertia or lack of belief in our gifts that keeps any of us from stepping forward and leading.

We owe the world something because of the nobility into which we are born. We are under an obligation to make something of ourselves. Otherwise, we are like the son of a billionaire who walks around with blank checks in his pocket but never uses them for anything worthwhile.

We are dealing with the conundrum of potential. As I said earlier in this chapter, we have more of it today than ever before in history.

CHAPTER
THIRTEEN

Making Potential Real

"Never forget that you are one of a kind. Never forget that if there weren't any need for you in all your uniqueness to be on this earth, you wouldn't be here in the first place. And never forget, no matter how overwhelming life's challenges and problems seem to be, that one person can make a difference in the world. In fact, it is always because of one person that all the changes that matter in the world come about. So be that one person. "
-Buckminster Fuller

There lives within us something nameless, something elusive—something dazzling and dangerous and disquieting. It sticks out a foot and trips us when we are trudging along in mundane routines. It rousts us from sleep and needles us into action. It finds us in the middle of what should be great contentment and sends us off on quests only don Quixote would understand.

What is this thing we can't quite touch, this waking dream that eludes the fingertips of our minds when we reach for it?

It is the voice of our truest Self. It is the impulse of Soul asking to be embodied. It is our potential crying out to be fulfilled.

The good news about potential is that Nature wants us to fulfill it. The bad news is that Nature is ruthless.

When I speak of Nature, I don't mean the great outdoors. Nature is Life, the Universe and Everything. Above and below. Within and without. The four winds. The four directions. Tension and slack. Sun, moon, and stars. Earth beneath our feet. Sky above our heads. Nature is everything that makes up our lives here on earth. All of it is speaking to us, guiding us, and dropping clues along the path using symbols and feelings. Coincidences, synchronicity, serendipities, encounters with strangers, inner nudges—we are always being guided if we pay attention.

Nature does not set about to make us comfortable or confident as we are growing into what we can become any more than it makes sure baby quail or fir seedlings survive the elements, though. In fact, if we go into the mountains and watch how things work, we will see tenderness and fierceness coexisting. A mother wolf will curl her body around her cubs to keep them warm, but later she will tear out a doe's throat with not a moment's hesitation.

We humans are the only creatures who believe that Nature should be kind to us and help us succeed. All the rest know that they are in a life-and-death dance with Her at every moment. They all seem to know without thinking about it that Nature will kill them if She can, but they still dance on, accepting Her gifts and hiding from Her fury if possible. We fool ourselves into believing that we have conquered Her with our machines and governments and roads. While we may not be as subject to the rain and wind as we once were, we must still deal with the implacable truth that Nature owes us nothing when it comes to bringing forth the best that lies within us.

Still, something in Nature abhors unrealized potential. She is the Great Mother and spreads herself out all around us to make our growth possible. Nature is personal and impersonal at the same time.

It is a paradox. On one hand, Nature cares nothing for our

comfort and happiness. On the other hand, She carries out the laws that govern everything and must therefore provide us with the raw materials we need to create anything we wish. It is our job to dig it out and use it.

Joseph Campbell said, *"The goal of life is to make your heartbeat match the beat of the universe, to match your nature with Nature."*

This is true and rings with a Taoist lyricism, but that matching of which he spoke is not as soft as it might sound. The process of tuning our heartbeat with Life is actually a fight to the death.

Like a fierce, magnificent lover, Life is not satisfied with forcing us to surrender to her. If we want peace of mind, we must learn to submit to Life and love her capriciousness; however, Life is also needling us, taunting us, turning away from us...driving us to the point of absolute exhaustion. She longs for the moment, when, lying flat on our backs and unable to move, we find our own savage, rebellious hearts.

When we tap an artery of strength and courage, when we rise up and fling Life backward against the wall and say, "No. Fuck you! I will not go down quietly. You can push me to my knees; I am bowed and bloody, but I am not beaten. Stand aside and watch, for I will not pass this way again"—at that moment, Life surrenders in admiration. It is what she wanted all along. She is a worthy adversary and sifts among the hearts of humankind to find a few who are strong enough to both surrender to her and also wrestle her down. To them, she gives everything. She will not yield her treasures easily or to any who lack the courage to go all the way.

In other words, Life is pleading with us to fully inhabit our own resplendent humanity. She wants us to listen to her heart, yes, but she is ravenous to strip us of everything necessary until she can hear the powerful drumbeat of our warrior hearts too. That is when, clawed and exhausted, we make love to Life and she to us.

In fact, we are the only creatures on this planet capable of this conscious, combat-romance with Life. It is woven into our nature and we alone occupy this layer of consciousness. That means we are important somehow—that the very quality of our being here this way matters. All other creatures on the spectrum of awareness simply go with the flow. They live and die and don't ask why. Not us humans. We are different among the others. Our entire existence is a great question. We are creators by birthright. I am forced to acknowledge that, even though we are often confused about what we are here for, our place on the continuum has its own purpose.

As I said early on, the greatest problem we face in this age is a question of purpose. We might also call this a question of "How do I live my destiny?"

I now see that we live our destiny by fulfilling the potential of our own unique design.

Imagine that an acorn has sprouted into a tiny oak seedling. After a year of surviving the sun and wind, it is six inches tall. Two years later, it stands two feet high. This little tree can eventually grow to over one hundred fifty feet in height, but it may take over a century to get there. If it were a human, it would probably watch a nearby bunch of bamboo shooting up a foot per day and have a nervous breakdown. It might develop severe depression and insecurity, or even try hard to make itself look like the bamboo in hopes of matching its speed.

That is ridiculous, of course—and we do it all the time when we compare ourselves to other people on our own path of destiny.

The oak tree uses all of its available resources—sun, water, and nutrients in the soil—to become itself. It digs deep into the earth and reaches toward the sky. It patiently stands there, growing and growing and growing, becoming more and more.

Success for anything or anyone is becoming what it was designed to be. That's it.

This is why we weird people need to perform a radical redefinition of success. We need to do this *now* so we aren't constantly knocked off course when we see someone else shooting up into fame and fortune and immediately assume that we must not be good enough, or are doing something wrong.

David W. Orr said this in his book, *Ecological Literacy: Educating Our Children for a Sustainable World:*

"The plain fact is that the planet does not need more successful people. But it does desperately need more peacemakers, healers, restorers, storytellers, and lovers of every kind. It needs people who live well in their places. It needs people of moral courage willing to join the fight to make the world habitable and humane. And these qualities have little to do with success as we have defined it."

Our culture hands out prizes to overnight success stories. We look at them, with their flashing smiles and adoring fans, and shrink into ourselves while an acid devil's cocktail of self-loathing and envy eats at our vitals.

There is nothing wrong with them. There is also nothing wrong with us. The quicker we get that, the quicker we will go back to work and pour all of our energy into what makes our spirits sing. When I say, "There is nothing wrong with them," I mean that they are doing what they do and it isn't our job to worry about why they are getting the prizes more quickly than we are. When we indulge in envy of others, we deny our own birthright that is this unique genius.

The trouble with this is that many of us have endured years of disappointment that have left us feeling unable to take the next step toward what makes us feel alive. Many Weird People have deep wounds left in us during childhood because we didn't fit in. Many were scoffed at and bullied school. Parents and teachers didn't understand us, so they tried to pound us into conventional molds, leaving our sensitive spirits crushed and bruised in the process. Most of them didn't mean to hurt us. Some were sadists, but most were just afraid that we wouldn't survive in the world with our weird ways and they felt helpless to do anything but try to force us to fit in. Many of us have not known how to bring the gifts we bear into the world from the fringes to which we felt banished.

Verily I say unto you that we are living in a new age. It is ripe and ready for us to find ourselves, be ourselves, and offer ourselves. We need to do it to be happy and the world needs us to do it. No one else is going to. They are too busy trying to be like everyone else.

We are living in the middle of a high renaissance. This means that we showed up on time with our weird, creative impulses.

Renaissances have peaked many times throughout history. Like ocean waves, human consciousness seems to rise and fall together. At times of rising, our potential is greater just because we were born during a high tide. We are living in just such a time at this very moment. All of us alive today are part of it, whether we know it or not.

Physicists use the term *potential energy*. It means that an object gains more stored energy as it rises or falls in relation to its position in the gravitational force field. A surfer has more potential energy at the crest of the wave than when she is floating along at sea level. A skier gains tremendous potential energy by taking a lift to the top of a mountain. Because his position is so high above the base line, gravity pulls down on his body and he can point his skis downhill and fly with almost no effort. We are living in the middle of the highest high water mark in human history—the greatest renaissance the world has ever known. You are and I am. All of us are. We are carried upward by the rising wave of which everyone is a part. Imagine that this wave is made up of over seven billion water molecules, and each one of them is a person. That is what is going on right now. We have more potential energy stored in us than people did fifty years ago. That's real power to get things done. We have all risen together to an extremely high high-point. The tension created by this energy is palpable.

The problem with potential energy in this example is that it can't be used for anything unless we are aware of it and know what to do with it. In fact, all that energy is making everyone feel crazy right now. Most people aren't aware of what is happening. They aren't living with purpose, and, as a result, the world is a barrel of dynamite waiting to blow up because most are in a total reaction mode. All that compressed energy could be used to blast a massive hole in the prison we have built for ourselves—or it could destroy everything. The difference is in how it is used.

During renaissance periods, creativity, personal freedoms, art, literature, science, and technology explode. Some humans harness the leverage of their age and produce things that change the world (for good or ill) forever after. Each high wave is followed by a low period. We have called those Dark Ages. During dark, low times, genius still finds a way to surface and shine, but it is much more difficult.

Overlay that idea on this earth age and we will see that each of us has enormous power. We have gained a high altitude as a species. Everything is moving faster. The pressure is much greater. We have seven billion people here—and that number has grown by almost six billion since the mid-1900s. We have shrunk the globe with our communications technology. Within a single generation, everything has exploded. The Internet has made it possible for us to work anywhere, create things out of thin air, sell to people around the world, and develop relationships with people we have never met. Information is surging around us at blinding speeds. We are cracking DNA codes and sending data over airwaves to print solid objects with 3-D printers. Things have accelerated to a stunning degree and the stakes have never been higher.

The great geniuses of the past solved problems of how to protect us from Nature and other humans. We have followed that path to a logical crossroads. We are as good as we will ever need to be at that sort of thing. It's time for a change of direction. The great geniuses we need now must solve the problem of hatred and of how to make love practical.

Pierre Teilhard de Chardin was a Jesuit priest, philosopher, and true renaissance man (and a heretic whose books were censored by the Catholic Church). He wrote, "Someday, after mastering the winds, the waves, the tides and gravity, we shall harness for God the energies of love, and then, for a second time in the history of the world, man will have discovered fire."

And this is where you and I come in, my dear fellow Weirdian. We are here to wake up and remember who we are. We are here to tune in to the call of our souls that is begging us to grow into our unique design. We are here to be examples of what is possible when a person does their most authentic thing. There is something that happens when people light up like this. They illuminate the space around them. They wake up other people who have been sleepwalking through life. Without even trying, they change the world—just by becoming their most turned-on, alive self.

That doesn't happen without first becoming aware of and then taking responsibility for our own potential. That is what we are here to do.

I love four words: Purpose, mission, potential, and destiny.

These are grand, inspiring, passion-inducing words. They blast like a trumpet in my spirit. They are also vague.

How do we find them?

What do we do with them?

Where do we go with them?

The path can only become clear by learning how to listen to the voice of Soul.

CHAPTER
FOURTEEN

The Call of Soul

"The soul is placed in the body like a rough diamond,
and must be polished, or the luster of it will never appear."
-Daniel Defoe

B efore we talk any more about ideas, I want to tell you a story. This
is called *The Temple of Dreams.*

In a faraway land and a time long forgotten, a wise and powerful
woman lived by herself in a mountain place. She had a cat and a
teapot named Lu.

Each year, people would walk for many miles through the snow
and wind to visit her. For she had built her house and lived there
quietly, but those who knew it called it the Temple of Dreams.

She refused all gifts and rarely opened the door to those who
knocked, but they came all the same.

Because everyone who found their way to the temple was allowed
to speak their fondest dreams aloud in the clear mountain air. It

mattered not whether the dreams were large or small--only that they were uttered from the most honest place within. Then they could write their hearts' desires on slips of paper, fold them into paper airplanes, and sail them into the winds that rushed and moaned around the hilltop.

The boldest pilgrims would sit for a long time and imagine themselves as if their very best dreams had already come true. Then, they would drink a dipper of water from the spring that always bubbled cold and pure nearby and ring the bell hanging from a twisted pine branch.

But one day, a man came knocking at the temple door. His feet were ragged from the journey and his beard had grown shaggy in ways that no one from his village would approve. He knocked three times and looked about but only heard the sighing wind and an eagle crying in the bright sky.

Because the holiday celebrations were occupying all those who lived in the valleys down below, he was alone at the temple door. He knocked three times again, but no answer came from the other side. Since there was nothing else to do, he sat on the stairs and ate a piece of cheese he had saved in the pocket of his robes.

A long while passed, but he did not leave. Instead, he sat and let the sunshine bathe his face and watched the eagle loop and soar above the mountaintops. Just before he would have set about to take his departure, he heard a cat's meow behind the door. It roused him from his reverie and he sprang to the door and knocked three times again.

Not certain he had heard anything at all, he pressed his ear against the door and listened. When it opened, he nearly fell inside but caught himself just before stumbling into the arms of the woman who stood within. She stared at him with a half smile, her dark hair falling around her shoulders with a few silver strands gleaming in the sunlight.

"What do you want?" she said. The cat peered up at him from between her feet.

"What?" he said, stammering. He had expected to leave this place empty-handed after all, but now the priestess stood there watching and he had to find the words to tell why he had taken the long journey.

"What do you want?" she said again.

He paused and looked down into the valleys filled with mist. He had read many things and studied the teachings of gurus far and near. From them, he had learned that desire was the root of suffering and that he should be happy with what he already had. He looked back into the amber eyes of the woman and said, "I don't know what I want."

"Then that is what you will get," she said and moved to shut the door. But the cat had crept forward to sit in a spot of sunlight and the woman had to choose between closing this stranger out or pinching her friend's tail.

"Wait," he said, "I have walked many miles to come here and I won't leave until you show me what must be seen."

A teapot shrieked from somewhere inside the dwelling, and she turned. "Come then. Lu has called and we mustn't keep her waiting. You can tell me a few things over a hot cup before you go."

He followed her into the warm entry, but she had already vanished around a corner and he could hear her muttering from another room. The cat stared at him while he straightened his hair and robes, then led the way ahead, tail straight and twitching slightly.

"They always want something, but not this one," he heard her saying to herself as he entered the snug kitchen. She was pouring hot water into cups, steam rising in a cloud around her head.

"Well, that's not entirely true," he said. "I do want something, or I wouldn't be here. It's just that I have become content with my things. I don't know what to ask."

She turned, holding a carved tray with little cups full of tea. "Come with me," she said and walked away toward windows that looked out over an infinity of space.

Once seated, she handed him a cup with a small bow. "So," she said, "you know many things, most of them very good. What you don't know is the most important and it is not something your books have told you."

"What is that?"

"Why don't you tell me again what you really want?"

"I want everything exactly as it is," he said. "I know that life unfolds to give me what is best."

"Ah, that's a lovely concept, but it still doesn't explain why you walked many miles and just ate your last scrap of food on my doorstep."

He shifted on his cushion and met her eyes. "Well, I have a house and comfortable things. I enjoy my work and appreciate my friends. I have everything a man should want except…"

"Except," she said. "Tell me the except. 'Except' is everything you have never dared to ask, and in that lies your destiny, your truth, and your happiness."

"Oh. Well, since I was a little boy, I have always wanted to write great stories. I have wanted to turn the things I saw and felt into words and share them with the world. I want to love a woman who will take long and foolish magical journeys with me. I know this won't make me happy but…"

She held up her hand. "Stop. You know no such thing. It is foolishness to suppose that you can be happy if you do not bring forth that which lies within. Forget your concepts and listen to me now."

The priestess sipped her tea. "Many people make the journey to this place each year. Most of them never knock and, if they do, I rarely answer. But you knocked three times. You will not be denied.

Everyone who comes receives something. Perhaps the journey here alone is reward enough for most. All return home changed because they allowed themselves to ask. We live in a fascinating universe, full of mystery and delight. Someone you may have heard of once said, 'For every one that asketh receiveth; and he that seeketh findeth; and to him that knocketh it shall be opened.' Does this ring a bell?"

He nodded.

"Good. You are here today to ask. Do that. Understand that what your truest self desires is not only good, but it is also well within your birthright to receive. You are not here today to mull over concepts. You have done that for far too long already. Most people who come here ask for things they don't really want. Sometimes they get a version of what they think they desire, but what they don't know is that Life serves up for us what we actually desire most—not what our mind has been pushed and tricked into believing. And the truth is, most are simply too afraid to ask for their deepest soul-desire. They will settle for a nicer home or a better job or a thousand other wishes that fall short of their insatiable hidden truth."

"Here," from inside her robe, she produced a small scroll and pen, "take this out to the step after you have done drinking your tea. Write down everything you would see come true in your life from this day forward. Leave nothing out. When you finish, hold it in your hands until you can see yourself in that picture you have created. Unlike the others who have journeyed here, I want you not to throw it into the wind. Instead, feel everything and then ring the bell. Then go back down the mountain and read your own new story every day. For you see, no one is waiting in the wind to make your dreams come true, but Everything will come to your aid if you do what I have told you."

And so saying, she kissed the man on his forehead and disappeared into some distant room while wind rang the chimes and sunlight turned an eagle's wings to silver in the sky.

After a long time, the man made his way to the doorstep and opened the scroll. Across the top were words written in red. "Anything you truly desire is possible. Write…"

I keep using the word Soul. Many people get nervous around it because they are sure it must have some religious or spiritual connotation. I am not interested in any definition other than the raw heartthrob of longing that has pulsed beneath the soundtrack of our lives since we were born. There are yearnings that have pulled us forward through every scene, keeping us on the search for something real—something that matches only itself. We can't be satisfied with anything less, no matter what we try to substitute for it. The voice of Soul can be heard when we pay attention to our true desires.

This tale I just shared offers a new beginning. It opens a door with that word "except." As the wise woman said, *"Tell me the except. 'Except' is everything you have never dared to ask, and in that lies your destiny, your truth and your happiness."*

It reminds me of what Jesus Christ is quoted as saying, "Unless you become as little children, ye shall not enter the Kingdom of Heaven." Imagine that the kingdom we seek is found by living out these soul cries. Now what if, like children who don't know better than to ask for what they truly want, we do that? What if we follow our dreams back to where they are rooted and find that they are innocent and necessary to pursue? If we do this, we will find our true brilliance. As Charles Baudelaire once said, "Genius is nothing more or less than childhood recaptured at will."

Sometimes when I talk about these things, people will object. "What about perverts and psychopaths?" they say. "They desire horrible things. What about them?"

I'm not talking about sick, twisted things that will harm others.

What comes from the truest part of us is always pure. There are personalities and minds so broken that the soul impulse becomes distorted and misdirected. I can't deny that. However, follow any desire back to where it originates and we will find simple things: a need for acceptance, a longing for love, a craving for home, a yearning to belong, a hope to feel safe.

Right now, if we want to hear the call of Soul and make it real in our own lives, the first step is to pay attention to our longings and what lies behind their obvious faces. It probably isn't just a finer home or a better paying career. Those are worthy, but they will not scratch the itch deeply enough. There is something more—something deeper. What is that? How would it like to be expressed in our lives, as us?

Dare to dream again.
For dreaming is the
language of your soul,
And nothing your soul truly desires
Could ever be wrong or impossible.

My friend, Janet Conner, is the author of the bestselling book *Writing Down Your Soul.* I am not exaggerating by saying that it changed my life. It still does. She teaches people to begin a deep dialogue with themselves that reveals everything in a completely safe space. What happens is mystical and so intimate that nothing is allowed but the truth that emerges during the process.

Janet says that the soul wants five things—

1. To Connect
2. To Commit
3. To Serve
4. To Express
5. To Create

As I spend time with each of these in my own life, I find that they are practical and also lead me to acknowledge the most important things for which I have ever hoped.

I ask myself, "How do I want to connect?" The answers show up as my pen moves across the page. These are not mystical concepts. They are what I desire to experience in this lifetime. I can't avoid or explain them away.

"How do I long to commit...serve...express...create?" When I ask these questions honestly of myself, the inner voice answers with equal honesty and practicality. The fog clears. I can't deny what is right before my eyes. Soul has spoken.

As we stay on this path, Soul gets bolder and more insistent. The vision gets clearer and more magnificent than what we dared to see before.

I am not attempting to write a self-help or how-to book. The world is already full of those and there are many great ones, some of which have shaped the course of my own life. Unlike books of that type, though, you won't find exercises at the end of each chapter. This is no exception. However, if you want to connect with the voice of your Soul, maybe it will help to find a quiet place with a notepad and pen and write out the honest dreams of your heart, leaving nothing out, just as the old priestess instructed her insistent pilgrim to do. It is a place to start. What are your "Excepts"?

CHAPTER
FIFTEEN

A Trail of Breadcrumbs

You have left a trail of breadcrumb clues
that will lead you to the place
where your purpose and passion
have already met and are simply
waiting for you to find them.

So, how do I find my purpose?

Now we are getting down to it. This is the part where we sit down right in the middle of our lives, take inventory, and ask, "What have I been doing and why doesn't it feel right?"

Creativity isn't a place we go or something we do; it is a way of life. It is who we are meant to be. We are creators. The primitive answer, "My purpose is to live," is simple, but the reason it doesn't quite satisfy us now is because that level of living is only experiencing what has already been created. If we don't feel a sense of purpose, it is because we are having a life experience of someone else's creations. We have agreed that their creation is better than ours could be, so we allow their work to take the place of our own. We do this when we over-consume television shows, movies, music, food, lifestyles, fashions, books, or anything else that keeps us from creating for ourselves. I love everything on that list. There is nothing wrong with any of them, but if we never create our own things in the space of life and merely fill it with the creations of others, it should come as no surprise when we feel empty. It does no good to work at a horrible job only for a paycheck, then spend our few leisure hours blowing the money on things we don't need and didn't create in an attempt to fill the void. We will not find any satisfaction in that.

Sometimes the only thing for it is to answer a question with a question. When we ask, "What is my purpose?", the most direct way to answer it is by asking, "What do I wish to create?"

This is a refined question and it is earthy. It doesn't allow us to get stuck in the clouds.

*When in brief flashes of
serendipity you glimpse
what you were born to do...
Do it.
No matter what.
Take steps toward it, even if they are
depressingly small at first.
With each inch closer to your
central magic, you will feel it.
It is unmistakable for anything else.
It's called purpose.*

I met with a client last night. Mark had attended a recent Creative UnBootcamp, which is my introductory class for aspiring writers. He followed this by scheduling intensive sessions with me in hopes of getting motivated to finish one of the many writing projects he had started over the years.

As we entered the sacred field of his hopes and dreams, I began to sense tremendous tension and static in him. He wanted to talk about writing, but a question kept pushing itself into the space between us—"What do you want to create?"

I asked it.

"Oh, you know, I want to write this book and things like that, but my job is killing me and I can't find the energy to be creative when I get home at night," he said.

Mark described his life. His work was frantic and he resented it. His family was filled with overachievers and he was the lone strange one who had never quite connected the dots. He felt isolated from the world, doubtful that he could overcome the pain of his past attempts and failures, and obligated to endure a lifestyle that left him depleted.

"What do you really want?"

"I want a different life!"

Something cracked then. That was the real issue. Mark has the power of a nuclear power plant, creatively speaking. I felt it every time we talked. He didn't need motivation. He needed to stop seeing his creativity as somewhere to go after all of his other duties were fulfilled.

"Tell me about that life. Paint me a picture. Walk me through a day in the life of Mark if you could have it exactly the way you want it."

It was hard at first. He began talking in general terms—big words, big concepts. I stopped him.

"No, Mark. I can't see that life. Those ideas are too fuzzy. Lead me through a day in the life you really want."

Then he did it. I felt him become a young boy, dreaming out loud about everything he desired to experience and become. The dam broke and he let it all out. There wasn't a single feature of his perfect life that was outlandish or impossible. Some of them were big goals, like becoming a staff writer for TV drama or comedy shows, but they weren't in a completely different galaxy. He got excited and started telling me about people he knows who could introduce him to working television writers and how they would give him pointers about how to get started. He began to describe his studio apartment in New York City and how he would walk to the subway and meet interesting people and spend his days in exciting work with a team of other creatives. He walked me home with him and, in our imaginations, ordered take-out at a little restaurant in his neighborhood. He told me about new friends and his new love relationship with a woman he had met as part of this picture. He explained that, because his life felt so good, he could go home and work on the novel and screenplays that had been gathering dust for so many years.

When he finished creating this picture of his life, he stopped talking for a while. Silence stretched between us for several long seconds. Then he said, "That's what I want. I have never been able to say it before."

I could feel his soul's thumb pressing down on the blank page of his future, leaving a unique print of itself—revealing the singular map of a life he wanted more than anything else.

We talked about that and also the breadcrumb clues he had been following all his life that had led him through so many disappointments to this place of clarity. He began to see that nothing had been wasted, that everything had conspired to move him in the direction of his purpose—even the things that had hurt. He told me that he had always had a hard time admitting what he wanted because he thought it needed to be so much bigger. He felt that his perfect life picture might be viewed as average by his highly accomplished family members. When he relaxed into the truth of himself, he felt immense relief—and so did I.

Mark's path winds on into the horizons of his destiny, but now he is actively watching for the breadcrumbs. He is engaged and focused on moving in the direction of his desires.

The major realization for me from this experience with another traveler is that we cannot put creativity in a sealed room and visit it sometimes when we have time and energy.

Being creative is not about being artsy; it is the rugged forever-commitment to carve a life that allows full expression of ourselves, however that looks. Defined this way, there can be no real success without creativity because anything less means living a poor, cramped life.

In other words, living creatively rescues us from the soulless existence that has swept across the world and makes the zombie pandemic in *The Walking Dead* look like just an average flu season. Most people in what we call first world countries are living lives that bear no resemblance to anything they really want. They have not used their imagination, energy, and intention to design a life that matches the thumbprint of their souls. Instead, they fall into patterns established for them by other creators. As a result, we are living in this time of great crisis during which most people stagger through their days lacking any sense of purpose. It matters because this creates an atmosphere ripe for the kind of despair that leads to terrorism, mass shootings, suicide, and other forms of human chaos.

The antidote for all of this is to find our own private trail of breadcrumb clues that lead us home to ourselves. It is also mingled with a great need to give these yearnings the kind of attention for which they have been begging all of our lives.

When we turn our focus toward them, we discover a marvelous new energy growing up within that makes it possible to take steps forward. With each step, more clues appear in the form of synchronicity, serendipity, bits of information, opportunities, and subtle inner nudges. Sometimes the strangest, least-likely-to-be-divine-messengers people show up with precisely what we need. All of these emissaries speak to us in the symbolic language of Soul and only wait on us to give them enough attention so that they can be translated into literal action that will transform our whole lives into creative works of art.

Living out a creative life means taking ultimate responsibility for everything in it. It means that we are not waiting for anyone or anything to come along and give us the keys to happiness. It also means that we become leaders by example of what is possible when an individual lives by their own lights.

And yes, it is weird to live this way because so few are doing it. It is also unspeakably worth the effort.

The poet, Nayyirah Waheed, says it this way —

"creativity keeps the world alive, yet, every day we are asked to be ashamed of honoring it, wanting to live our lives as artists. i've carried the shame of being a 'creative' since i came to the planet; have been asked to be something different, more, less my whole life. thank spirit, my wisdom is deeper than my shame, and i listened to who i was. i want to say to all the creatives who have been taught to believe who you are is not enough for this world, taught that a life of art will amount to nothing, know that who we are, and what we do is life. when we create, we are creating the world. remember this, and commit."

CHAPTER SIXTEEN

What If I Fail?

*"No great deed, private or public,
has ever been undertaken in a bliss of certainty."*
— Abraham Maslow

The specter of failure is among the hardest things to face when we turn toward the voice of our true selves and begin to dream again. Many Weird People have suffered tremendous disappointment in life, and some have experienced almost nothing else. A steady diet of being misunderstood, not fitting in, working ill-suited jobs, and other difficulties makes it hard for many of us to believe that we can find a solid place in this world. As a result, we may make the mistake of accepting far less than the joy, fulfillment, and abundance that are written into our birthright.

When we ask, "What if I fail?" we are forgetting how much we love thrillers and dramas—as long as they are about other people. The tales that captivate us the most show characters driven to the brink of disaster. We absolutely love these stories. They all contain the element of risk and uncertainty. That is what makes them exciting.

"Will he get the girl?"

"Will she get the boy?"

"Will he survive the battle?"

"How will they overcome that?"

"Can she solve the mystery in time?"

"Can they steal the jewels and escape before the police show up?"

On and on it goes. Without the element of impending death, disaster, or failure in some form, we would be bored—like knowing exactly how the movie ends before we start watching. It is the same way in our quest to live our dreams. If we knew for sure that we would succeed in our mission, it would not have enough intrigue to seduce us into the kind of tangles that call forth our best stuff. It is a paradox. What might destroy us is exactly what is required to make us find our finest qualities. One isn't possible without the other. Our greatest wound is on the flip side of the coin from our greatest gift to the world. Joseph Campbell said, "The cave you fear to enter holds the treasure you seek."

Go look at the history of nearly every person known for some great work and you will find a trail of tears, abuse, hardship, or handicaps that forced them to seek the cure for their pain. Their search led them to their own genius. Could they have found and revealed it otherwise? It is hard to say. What is certain, though, is that we can find those clues we need—the map to our own purpose—by looking into our own shadow and feeling our way to joy, one step at a time.

Uncertainty is a necessary ingredient for transformation—which is why most people would rather stick with what they are sure about rather than step into an unknown future, regardless of its promise of greatness.

As Anaïs Nin said, "It takes courage to push yourself to places you have never been before... to test your limits... to break through barriers. And the day came when the risk it took to stay tight inside the bud was more painful than the risk it took to blossom."

And sometimes it's necessary to stop running from the fear of failure and just turn around to face this demon ghost. It can transform everything...

Eric read my first book and contacted me out of the blue. We both lived in Boise, so I got the unusual pleasure of meeting one of my readers in the flesh.

We met for beers and he began to pour out his story. He was running his own insurance business and working hard to achieve goals, but he was terrified by a sense of being far off course. He was doing everything right—making sales calls, servicing clients' needs, attending business leads groups, and a hundred other tactics that all the experts told him would work. Nothing was working. He was making a living, but he was internally desperate. He knew he wasn't living his own purpose and he didn't know what to do about it.

Like many who have read the book, he was also concerned that the only way to shift gears would require a radical burn-down of everything he had built. That was never the message I intended to convey, but people have often identified with parts of my story and fear that perhaps the only way to move into a life-on-purpose is some kind of drastic meltdown.

As we talked, Eric told me that he was reading everything he could get his hands on about personal growth and transformation. He was meditating, visualizing, vision boarding, brainstorming, and goal setting. We spent a few hours together and agreed that we should hang out in the future to compare notes. I asked him to see me as a fellow traveler and take only the parts of my story or advice I might offer under the advisement of his own soul.

I watched the relief in his eyes grow as he realized that I wasn't handing him a map. I wasn't telling him he needed to do it like I had. In fact, I was asking him to disregard anything from my experience that didn't feel useful or right for him.

Over the next year, we occasionally took long walks by the Boise River. We wandered along the greenbelt, smoked cigars, and talked for hours. I sensed that he was approaching his own crossroads. The closer he got, the more anxiety he revealed during our times together. He started applying for jobs outside his industry, trying to imagine how he could make the leap into something more aligned with his inner direction. His fear was tangible and came out in stories of visualized disaster. Eric had been doing a lot of personal work and was conscious that the "monkey mind" was running him ragged. He hated that he couldn't control his thoughts and hold an inspiring vision of his own future. He knew better, but that didn't seem to matter. His emotional needle made wide swings. Sometimes he would call me and say that he was going to buckle down, give up wild dreams of a different life, and just make things work on his current path. Other times, he would tell me that he was ready to walk away from everything no matter what.

One day, I was nudged to lead him through a process. Rather than keep trying to imagine a mysterious and wonderful future, I felt that he needed to explore the awful things that could happen if he tried but failed in epic fashion.

"Eric, let's say that you step away from your current job and try a new venture," I said.

"Okay?"

"Tell me something. If it doesn't work out, what happens next?"

"Well, I would run out of money pretty fast."

"And then what would happen?"

"I would probably freak out."

"No, I mean, what would happen in your life?"

"Oh, I would dip into my credit cards and start running up a lot of debt while I tried to find another job."

"What about if you couldn't find a job and had no credit left?"

"I guess I wouldn't be able to pay my bills. They'd come take my car and my house would go into foreclosure. I would have to beg money from friends or go on food stamps to keep my kids fed."

"How would you feel about that?"

"It would be horrible. I would feel like such a failure."

"How would your wife react?"

"I don't know. I mean, she's a good woman, but I'm not sure she could handle that. She might divorce me and take the kids."

"Is that the worst thing that could happen?"

"Yeah. I mean, I can't even imagine being in that situation."

"What would you do then?"

"Oh, man…I have no idea. I would be so destroyed that I might crack. I might end up homeless and have to hold a sign on the corner begging money from strangers."

"Would you die?"

"I might wish I was dead, but no… I wouldn't die."

"Is there any way you could come back from that if everything you just told me happened? Tell me how that might look."

Then he started to plot an imaginary comeback. Step by step, he told me how he would make small, resourceful choices to rebuild his life. I felt him enter a new place of peace. He had taken a journey into the depths of personal hell and discovered that even if the worst possible scenario happened, he would still have his life and his power of choice. He could start over. He could overcome.

"Eric, none of that needs to happen. You know that, right?"

He got excited and began telling me all about what he was going to do the next day. I watched him transform from a man in a state of confusion and fear into a powerful, creative force.

By temporarily dropping his shields of optimism and positive thinking and imagining the worst, he empowered himself. He began to access the infinitely potent creator matrix. He could do this because he took his own virtual journey through the valley of death. When he discovered that even the worst couldn't kill him, he defanged the serpent of his own fears.

Shortly afterward, a new opportunity showed up and Eric acted on it. He quit his soul-killing job and launched the project with a local entrepreneur. It required all of his skill, intelligence, and resilience, but the next time we met, I was in the presence of a man on fire. He was leaning across the raw edge of his fear, living into his own dream, and he knew it.

Eric is creating his own picture now rather than living cramped inside an old one painted for him by others.

When people ask, "How do I live my soul purpose?", what they often mean is, "Can you guarantee that I won't lose anything on this journey?"

They are asking for a promise that they can change their life but avoid the pain of change. They want to know that the identity they have been maintaining will stay intact.

Here is the hard truth: there are no guarantees. Well, actually, there is a guarantee. We will lose things.

The promise is that if we follow our hearts, live our purpose, and transform into the people we are capable of becoming, we will lose everything that doesn't serve our highest good.

But what loss is that?

It gets ridiculous when we look at it this way: "My life, minus everything that doesn't help me, equals my greatest potential and fulfillment."

There is no easier math.

JACOB NORDBY

Learning how to work this equation belongs here because loss and failure are so closely related in our minds. Lose a job, lose a friend, lose a house, lose a lover, lose our wallet or keys—all of those bring up feelings of failure. We wonder, "What did I do wrong?" If we don't care about something, it doesn't matter if it goes away. Only those things we cherish trigger fear of failure when we consider losing them or not accomplishing them.

Trying to express our deepest truth in life—and by that I mean living out a life that reflects who we really are—is usually a crooked path with many switchbacks, dead end adventures, and hot, thirsty marches. Since we can't see the end from the beginning, it's common to feel lost most of the time.

In the *Misfits* chapter, we talked about Reluctant Heroes—ordinary men and women with wounds or chaos in their past who are called into heroic action by circumstances, despite their own feelings of doubt and misgiving. Every one of us who answers the inner call to live in full after enduring a lifetime of pain and disappointment is a Reluctant Hero. We might not feel that we have the necessary strength or passion to succeed, but something in us is relentless about getting back up one more time.

In his book *The Spice of Life*, M.H.S. Pourri wrote, "At any given moment, you have the power to say, 'This is not how the story is going to end.'"

Yes. Exactly.

*You know how every once in a while
you do something
and the little voice inside says,
'There. That's it.
That's why you're here' ...
and you get a warm glow in your
heart because you know it's true?
Do more of that.*

There are Weird People who have been so beaten down over time that they can't imagine finding enough scraps of optimism to fuel another try.

I have been there too. There have been a few times in my life during which I couldn't stomach one more optimistic quote. Even encouraging words from well-meaning people were painful to hear. Nothing seemed to apply to me or to my situation. Sometimes getting out of bed to handle the most mundane tasks felt like the equivalent of climbing a mountain. Living through these times was excruciating, especially since I saw myself as a positive person. I remember telling someone close to me after going through the loss of businesses I had built, "The only thing I regret losing is my optimism." Without that spark, I felt like I had lost my legs.

During that time, I met a man who has become a dear friend. Paul Boynton is the author of *Begin with Yes* and leads a tribe of well over one million fans on Facebook. I wasn't ready for someone to tell me that "Everything's going to be wonderful. Just get up and try again!" Paul didn't. Instead, he listened to me. He shared his own experiences of pain and failure in a way that made me sure he understood what I was going through. Then he gave me gentle encouragement to dream again and to take just a few simple steps forward. Little by little, as I took his advice, I felt the ground become solid beneath my feet. Then opportunities and resources started showing up—often in ways that are hard to describe as anything less than magical. One day at a time, my inner optimist recovered.

Now I enjoy a much stronger foundation of optimism, but it is not based on having a life without failures in my history. Going through my own heartbreaks has given me deep compassion for anyone who is not sure that life is worth living.

Just as I hoped people wouldn't when I was going through tremendous pain, I will never try to talk someone out of what they are feeling, but I do love to pay the gift forward, passing along what Paul Boynton and some other dear ones did for me. They are real life examples of what Albert Schweitzer once wrote: *"In everyone's life, at some time, our inner fire goes out. It is then burst into flame by an encounter with another human being. We should all be thankful for those people who rekindle the inner spirit."*

It is a fact that Life is optimistic. I don't mean to anthropomorphize all over the Universe and suggest that it has mood swings or a human-like personality. That is soft-headed. What I do mean is that the principle of Life itself is optimistic. It keeps going. It keeps becoming. The life force causes seeds to crack open beneath mounds of dirt, sprout into the sunlight, and produce fruit, despite the risk of being killed by frost or wind. It fills humans with the desire to make love and give birth to babies, even in a world that is full of good reasons not to do that. Life keeps making more of itself. Its creative urges are often met with failure, but, more often than not, it succeeds.

Weird People must recover optimism. We also need to remember that optimism is a by-product of creating. In other words, we gain more energy to finish a project by starting it, even when we feel the least confidence in our abilities. Life expands in marvelous ways when we take the first steps forward. It's the principle of inertia: "A body in motion tends to stay in motion; a body at rest tends to stay at rest." When we break out of inaction and take the smallest steps toward creating a work-of-art life, we gain power to do more of the same. Our energy grows, our dreams expand, and the resources we require to gain momentum show up in the strangest ways, exactly when they are needed. As Paul Boynton said to me years ago, "I hope you won't believe these words, but test them in real life." On days when we simply can't face our music or writing or whatever our art is, we can look around the rest of our lives and find some small (but tangible) action to take that will prove to ourselves that we are creators and have the power to craft a life worthy of that stubborn Something that won't let go within.

I am confident that this is exactly what the brilliant-but-tormented Nobel Prize winner Albert Camus was talking about when he wrote this letter,

My dear,

In the midst of hate, I found there was, within me, an invincible love.

In the midst of tears, I found there was, within me, an invincible smile.

In the midst of chaos, I found there was, within me, an invincible calm.

I realized, through it all, that…

In the midst of winter, I found there was, within me, an invincible summer.

And that makes me happy. For it says that no matter how hard the world pushes against me, within me, there's something stronger – something better, pushing right back.

Truly yours,
Albert Camus

CHAPTER SEVENTEEN

Rebel Magicians

"You have a right to experiment with your life. You will make mistakes. And they are right too. No, I think there was too rigid a pattern. You came out of an education and are supposed to know your vocation. Your vocation is fixed, and maybe ten years later you find you are not a teacher anymore or you're not a painter anymore. It may happen. It has happened. I mean Gauguin decided at a certain point he wasn't a banker anymore; he was a painter. And so he walked away from banking. I think we have a right to change course. But society is the one that keeps demanding that we fit in and not disturb things. They would like you to fit in right away so that things work now."
~ Anais Nin

Driving my teenage twins to school this morning, I pushed the power button on the stereo. Pink Floyd's *Dark Side of the Moon* started playing. *Thump...thump...thump...thump.* The first track starts with a drum sequence that sounds like a heartbeat. Outside my car, the winter morning was dark and wet; lines of cars carrying people to school, to work—mostly to places where they will sit in little boxes all day long, robotically doing things they haven't thought much about. Like most high school freshmen, my kids aren't interested in deep philosophy first thing in the morning, so I kept my thoughts to myself. My mind took wing and flew overhead, though. Pink Floyd sang on, giving words to the nameless desperation that haunts us in this world we have created—a world of boxes and cubicles and endless meetings and false urgency to do things we don't give a shit about. We have schizophrenic voices in our heads all day long. One of them says, "I don't want this. Stop it. Get out of here." Another says, "Sit down, shut up, and do your job. Who are you kidding? This is a life sentence, dude. Get used to the hard time. You ain't going nowhere..."

We definitely do not want that.

What we really want is magic. Like alchemists turning lead into gold, we want to take the current circumstances of our lives and transmute them into treasure. We want to harness our own power and that of the Universe to help us make our dreams come true. We also want to pay our bills, go out to eat sometimes, and take vacations. At times, the ideas of living an inspired life and one that works in the real world seem to war against each other. I am convinced that it is no longer an either-or choice.

This age on earth makes it possible for those of us who live in free societies to get radically creative and design lives that match our desires. We have a buffet of options before us but to feed ourselves from it, we have to get clear and then make decisions that may not keep a normal lifestyle intact.

As Osho said, "Creativity is the greatest rebellion."

This is where we are called upon to tap our subversive genius and figure out how to fucking change the game. Albert Camus said it best: "The only way to deal with an unfree world is to become so absolutely free that your very existence is an act of rebellion."

That sentence rocked my world when I first read it. It still does. When I bring it up in conversation, I watch a spark of hope ignite in people's eyes. It always makes me sad to watch that tiny rebel flame get extinguished under an avalanche of thoughts like "Yeah, but you can't do that in the real world. You've always wanted to get real, get free, and do your thing, but it's never worked. You just aren't one of those people. Get back in line, kid."

There is a way, though. There just is.

I have met many people over the last few years who woke up, decided that they were done trying to maintain lives that didn't suit them, and then changed things—sometimes in dramatic fashion.

Some of my friends have sold most of their stuff, built tiny houses, and enjoy a minimalist lifestyle that requires very little income to maintain. This opens a lot of space to travel, socialize, and work on their creative projects.

Others have cut the tether and are living in travel trailers. One of my best friends just did this. He was a world-traveling executive in the software industry. It would have been easy for him to keep earning a huge salary and work for another decade before retiring, but he chose to downsize early. He quit his job, sold his house, and reduced his possessions to what would fit in the trailer and a small storage unit back home. Now he is exploring the country and listening to the call of soul about what comes next. He recently told me what a challenge it was to dismantle the visible and invisible structures of his old life. He is exploring the outer world with his truck and travel trailer, and he is exploring his inner wilderness at the same time.

A number of people I know have quit long careers, cut their lifestyles to the bone, and gone back to college. They are recreating themselves. This kind of transformation requires enormous courage. They would not be doing it if they weren't clear on exactly what they want for the rest of their lives. Check that. They might not even be completely sure where they are going, but they know they have to follow the urgent call of their heart into something real. They have the guts to trust that they will figure it out if they move in the direction of that voice.

It is funny how much reaction these people get from those who have no desire to step off the normal track. Many are secretly envious, of course, but it is common for my adventurous friends to endure diatribes from other people about being responsible, midlife crisis, and all the usual yammer that unfree minds quote like scripture. It takes a certain rebelliousness to stop doing what everyone else is in favor of what works for us.

My point is not that we should all become minimalists either. Some of us love big homes and more rooted lifestyles. Socrates, another weird person from ancient times, said, "The unexamined life is not worth living." The real questions are "Who am I?" and "What do I want?"

Most people never ask those questions. As a result, they fall into the answers offered by advertisers, their social set, and the culture as a whole. They will be well regarded by their peers, but they won't experience high magic in life.

In our Formula for Real Magic, the first thing is to know ourselves. Next, we ask what we truly desire. In my experience, this is a dance between the two. Knowing ourselves is an enormous project and we can never finish it in one lifetime. The more we know, the more there is to discover. That's a daunting prospect, but if we turn Socrates's statement around, it might say, "The examined life is ridiculously worth living."

Examination is the key. "Who am I and what do I truly desire?"

To become rebel magicians and harness our power to create, it is critical to do a full inventory. That might look like this:

Step One: What is in my life now?
Step Two: What do I no longer want in my life?
Step Three: What do I want in my life more than anything?
Step Four: What am I willing to do to transform?

In my former business days, I read a book titled *The Blue Ocean Strategy.* The authors studied companies that had broken out of their industries' molds and created something new from what had been stagnant. They discovered a pattern of questions these companies asked about their offerings.

What will we offer more of?
What will we do less of?
What can we cut out altogether?

We can use either set of questions—or both of them—to bring our lives into radical focus and make creative decisions.

If we are honest with the process, we will get the information we need. The data is right there in black and white after we answer these questions. What we do with the answers is the tricky part.

These answers will make us face old things, big things, and hard things. We may discover that it is time for a marriage to end, or that a career must change, or social circles need to be abandoned. We may admit that it is time to lose weight, sell the boat, or quit drinking.

There is no one picture that represents a template of the perfect life for all of us. In fact, what rebel magicians have learned is how to cast their own visions and then step into them. I love how Leo Babauta says it: "Instead of focusing on how much you can accomplish, focus on how much you can absolutely love what you're doing."

It's easy to get stuck in the no-man's land between what we don't want anymore and what we desire most. Taking the first step toward what we want will reveal the path, usually an inch at a time.

There came a time after almost twenty years of marriage when I knew that it was going to end. I had known it for more than a decade, but I had not come to the crossroads before that point. I was terrified. This went against everything I thought myself to be—a good husband, a good father, and a good man. I didn't know how to take a step. Everything looked impossible. Finances, childcare, and too many other important details overwhelmed me. After a lot of soul searching, I realized that the only legitimate action was to have honest conversations with my then-wife. Looking back, it seems self-evident, but at the time, I was in such turmoil that this came as a revelation. None of it was easy, but with each conversation, I gained clarity. Circumstances arranged themselves in ways I could not have predicted. My greatest fears did not come true. With each honest step forward, the path rose to meet my feet in most unexpected ways.

As I witness my children now, living in a new home with their mother and stepfather, I'm frankly amazed. Somehow, they are getting exactly what they need and I couldn't have imagined it turning out as it has. Their stepdad is a man quite different than I am, and even that fact is providing critical puzzle pieces to round out their development. I don't want to cover this with a thick coat of Pollyanna paint because the waters have been rough at times. Every one of my fears, insecurities, and weaknesses came forward to be faced. Learning to lean into all of that discomfort and uncertainty has also taught me to pay attention to what I need. Anyone looking on might have noticed that I was so busy trying to be sure that everyone else was cared for that I wasn't able to be honest about what I needed. Of course, I couldn't see that until I was living alone for the first time in my entire life. In the absence of taking care of others, I had to tune in to the long-ignored voice of myself. All of this has served to invite me into occupying my own life more completely and with greater honesty about who I am.

I didn't know it back in the days before taking that rugged step forward, but this book wouldn't have happened had I not done it. It would have remained alongside many other deep desires gathering dust on the shelves of my imagination. As I look backward—and forward—now I realize how nothing important to my true self would be possible without honesty and action. I cannot create anything worthwhile from behind a safe façade that keeps a tidy image intact but allows me to deny what's real and raw and alive in me.

Magic is first in knowing ourselves,
Next, what we truly desire,
Then, giving ourselves permission
To go for it with a whole heart

Honesty turns out to be a critical ingredient for real magic in life—honesty with ourselves and with others. Honesty requires us to look at things with new eyes and gives birth to responsibility, which, in turn, draws us into our creative power to make the inevitable changes.

As I face the raw edge of my life these days, I frequently ask myself this question, "What is the most honest thing I can do right now?" The answer to that question always appears, and it is always my best next step.

CHAPTER
EIGHTEEN

Raw and Sexy

"When you make music or write or create, it's really your job to have mind-blowing, irresponsible, condomless sex with whatever idea it is you're writing about at the time."
-Lady Gaga

There is no way to finish a book of this type without talking about sex—at least a little bit.

The thing is, art is sexy. Creativity is sexual. Sex is the energy of creation itself. They are inextricably bound together and certain wisdom traditions tell us that they emanate from the same "chakra" or energy center in the body.

And, of course, sex isn't just a matter of fitting body parts together. Sex is the collision of worlds, galaxies, universes, souls, birds, and bees, and … everything.

A person with great creative energy is likely to have above average sexual energy too. How they express (or repress) that may or may not be with another human, but it's still there beneath the surface, boiling away and generating enormous power.

I find it fascinating to notice that creatives down through history have had a painful, complicated relationship with sexuality. Many artists have suffered persecution or, at the very least, tremendous misunderstanding for their sexual expressions.

Many poets, writers, painters, and actors were stuck with the label "libertine." It's odd that a word that shares a root with "liberty" could carry a pejorative ring. In classical times, syphilis was so common among musicians that it was known as "the composer's disease."

There's something about the non-linear, sensing/feeling, passionate, uninhibited bohemian nature of most Weird People. It won't be nicely boxed or stuffed into tidy little containers. It can also cause a tremendous amount of fear and shame in life until we figure out how to get clear, honest, and free with our sexy selves.

In this time of the new renaissance, we are presented with more and greater opportunities to express our art and genius—and the world we live in is increasingly tolerant of sexual preferences that would have been deemed (at least) aberrant in other times.

So what does this mean do us?

It means that it's time to get real, raw, and sexual.

Being human means being sexual. Both things—humanity and sexuality—also mean being constantly entangled in complication.

Entanglement and complication. We often use those words as if they are bad ones.

As if having deep, tangled roots is somehow wrong.

Of course the great, soaring part of us (I call it Soul) knows flight and weightlessness. It fears the snares of earth for good reason.

But once conscious of this—once aware that we can free ourselves over and over again, no matter what—the only thing for it is to relish entanglement. Root deeply in the rich, dark earth of being ourselves; these strange, heavy, beautiful, temporary human creatures.

For everything fought against grows. Everything denied or disowned

becomes more powerful. Everything hidden will reveal itself in darker ways.

And all that is embraced is liberated.

Liberated. That's what we want.

We want rich, free lives. We want to feel the fire and passion that comes with taking our leashes off and walking our own true paths with heart.

Many Weird People have struggled with a world that judges them harshly for stepping outside the sexual lines drawn by society. As with most of the other judgments leveled at us, this is because our insistence on getting and staying real makes us honest with our behavior. Where our behavior deviates from what is commonly accepted, society reacts out of fear.

What is considered right or wrong sexually lands at the very roots of our deepest, most powerful collective beliefs about survival and scarcity.

In *Prometheus Rising*, Robert Anton Wilson says, "Human society as a whole is a vast brainwashing machine whose semantic rules and sex roles create a social robot." He also explained that when you take an anthropological look at human sexuality around the world and backwards through time, the only "normal" is that one's tribe dictates how sexuality is expressed. In other words, every imaginable pairing or configuration is considered perfectly healthy, perfectly normal, depending upon the rules of that particular tribe. In some times and places, rulers were required to marry their sisters, for example. In others, multiple wives or multiple husbands were the norm.

I am not advocating any particular practice here. Nor am I promoting reckless, irresponsible behavior.

But ...

Here we are, living in a time on earth that offers us the opportunity to find pleasure in life, pleasure in creating, pleasure in exploring sexuality—and our era serves all of this on a platter. As with the other earmarks of this new renaissance in which we are living, the world has never seen anything like this on such a widespread scale at any time in (more or less) verifiable history.

Powerful creative people exude this tremendous sexuality—others are drawn to them because of this energy in their work and because of the indefinable, invisible sexual radiance that shines from them. Remember watching Prince on stage and how his presence commanded your attention—your desire for whatever the special "it" was that he had? Have you heard the tales of the ravenously brilliant Picasso and Albert Camus? Pick any of the shining stars from the galaxy of human creators and you'll know what I mean.

Think about this. Sex isn't part of life. Sex IS life. The eyes you are using to read these words came about because two humans had sex. This isn't something we can lock up in the bedroom. As Mark and I discovered together in our session, to which I referred earlier, creativity wasn't a place to go or something to do as separate from his "normal life." Neither is sex. Like it or not, we are energetic beings and we are always emanating and receiving sexual impulses. This happens all day long, all the time. When we engage in creating anything, we are tapping into that sexual-creative turbo force.

Sexuality and creative genius—they are inseparable. Also, in many cases, the artists themselves are not free to cast more than a sideways glance at the power of what they feel, but it colors their music or writing or paintings so deeply that you can't tell one from the other. A rainbow can't be what it is without the hues it paints across the sky. Neither can we express or create without refracting the great sexual-creative nature of the universe itself into the colors we display for others to see and feel. Art and the artist are sensual in the most inseparable sense.

But we are taught shame about this. We are taught to hide this force in us that carries the fierce cheerfulness of a summer thunderstorm. We are taught to push all of this back into shadow closets or under the bed where it can't do anything but become a weak, twisted version of itself.

I don't know exactly how we should resolve this tension—how we should raise the curtains and free ourselves to play in the great, unashamed dance of creation. It is a puzzle.

It is a puzzle worth solving.

When we solve what it means to be ourselves (and free ourselves to be that), something magical happens. There's that word again: magic. But it is magical. It is high magic to leap the fences that once held us in a cramped little prison of other people's opinions and run pell-mell toward the horizon of our own destiny.

I don't care if you are hetero-, bi-, homo-, pan-, trans-, or asexual. How you handle yourself with other people, so long as you are honest about what's true inside and treat others with respect in the process— it's all good.

In fact, it's more than "all good." Getting real and honest sexually is 100% critical to your success as a whole human being. It is liberating to stand up and speak the truth of who and how we are, regardless how that appears.

I have had the heart-opening experience of being near several people who were in the process of coming out about their sexuality. In every single case, they were terrified to show themselves. Also, every single time they did it, they were stunned to find out that they weren't alone, that they weren't killed, and that (in fact) there was a large group of other humans with similar preferences ready to welcome them.

It is time to get over, under, through, or around the boulders of shame that have blocked the path to being who we really are. That's because the world is now ready for it. Indeed, the world is begging for it.

When any of us gets real and gets free, it cuts one more painful old leash from the world's neck.

And, as I have discovered so clearly in my own life, there is absolutely no way to be a whole, happy creator without jumping right into the taboo waters of sexuality and learning how to swim. Learning to swim means becoming responsible. It means becoming kinder and more honest with ourselves and other people.

In fact, after I left religion behind, I needed to develop some kind of personal ethic—something stripped down to the bare wire. I needed a north star that did not rely upon a complicated belief system for its constant place as my guide. The ancient pagan dictum states, "And it harm none, do as ye will." I worked that one through my system and decided that it would stand the test of most things. Since then, I have rewritten it for my own personal doctrine.

I am here to live my life in freedom and leave the world better for having passed through this place.

The only way to leave the world in worse shape than I found it is to take from another what they can't or won't give of their own free will.

The reverse is true too. I do the world and myself wrong if I allow others to take what I do not wish to give. Of course, there are times when others will take something by force, but it is up to me to speak up and stand up.

As it turns out, this is an extremely high standard and requires tremendous honesty to live it out. We occupy a world that has operated for a long, long time on a system in which the weak must give up to the strong. This goes deeper, then, because the weak often play co-dependent games and take back from the strong in dishonest ways with a sense of justification.

What I'm talking about here is an entirely different way to live. I'm talking about what don Miguel Ruiz teaches in *The Four Agreements*—"Be Impeccable With Your Word."

This applies in intimate relationships and at work and in the family and in every other area too.

When we do this sexually, we break ancient chains of fear and shame that have been holding humanity captive since before we can remember.

If you want to test this and feel how hot the flame of honesty burns, try it next time you are tempted to play some kind of shadow game to get sex, to get a raise, or to get attention.

Ask, "… if I told the simple truth about my needs and desires in this moment, what would happen?"

Pull that thread a few times and it will begin to unravel many, many lies that are wound so tightly around all of our minds. We so easily believe that there is not enough love, sex, money, food, or attention to go around. What if that's not true?

What if the actual truth is that we can have whatever we need if we offer our own selves to the world freely and ask from it exactly what we desire?

What if there is plenty and we do not need to play any twisted little games to get more than enough?

The radical truth is that living this way changes everything. It challenges everything. It allows no unquestioned lie to sit there like a fat parasite sucking our vital life force and stealing the pleasure we deserve.

I am saying the following simple things:

Sexuality and creativity can't be separated—they are the same energy.

The world has had a twisted, fucked-up way of dealing with sex. We deserve better.

The only way we get better is to get honest.

When we get honest, we get free.

When we get free, we unleash our creative nature and our pleasure in all of life.

CHAPTER
NINETEEN

Leading the New Renaissance

"Don't ask yourself what the world needs, ask yourself what makes you come alive. And then go and do that. Because what the world needs is people who are alive."
-Howard Thurman

We are living in the greatest renaissance in human history. It comes with special privileges and responsibilities for those of us who wake up in the middle of it rather than sleep walk through it. We are offered freedom to create and express ourselves like never before. As we discussed previously, this age gives us massive leverage. It would be a tragedy—a colossal waste of every bit of evolution that has brought us to this point—if we don't step up to the challenge. In my imagination, I see the billions of people from generations past and the trillions of the future crowded around us, holding their breath. They are all waiting to see what we will do during this unique time on Earth.

Years ago, struggling with the enormity of the world's problems and feeling terribly discouraged about any chance of figuring the whole mess out, I picked up Abraham Maslow's book, *The Further Reaches of Human Nature.* On one hand, I was feeling the gravitational pull into giving it all up and going back to answering my personal question of purpose by making money and enjoying a comfortable life. But some tiny strand of electric wire stayed alive inside, prickling and sizzling with the question of "what if?" When I began to read Maslow's fascinating ideas, a light bulb popped in my spirit. Here was a man who wasn't afraid to (as he described it) keep throwing hunches out ahead of him and then working like hell to find out if they were true. He also acknowledged the risk of expending his entire life's work on fool's gold ideas. I liked him!

Maslow was a psychologist and pioneered research in human motivations—what makes us tick. He developed an ascending scale of needs that motivate people depending upon their overall circumstances. At the lowest end of this scale are the basic physical needs of the human animal—breathing, food, water, sex, sleep, homeostasis, and excretion. When those needs are met, we naturally seek higher order needs such as safety, love, belonging, and esteem. In his model, the highest level of need is self-actualization.

In fact, actualization is the big one—the last real frontier. We have already solved most of the greatest questions of the lower level needs, but we keep bumping our heads against actualization and then trying to ease our pain by returning to what used to satisfy our quest.

Self-actualization contains morality, creativity, spontaneity, problem solving, lack of prejudice, and acceptance of facts. In other words, when a human feels that they are safe and fulfilled on the other levels, they naturally want to answer the bigger questions. They seek to transcend what once occupied all of their time and energy.

This self-actualization thing simply means taking ultimate responsibility as the creators of our own lives—including the world in which we live.

It means growing up, taking back our own true power, and using it responsibly.

We have spent a lot of centuries working hard to build societies and systems that help us obtain physical safety and comfort. For most of us, that box is checked. We have also invested enormous energy by creating environments in which we can meet our higher-order needs—things like private property, social safety nets that keep people from dying of starvation, medical care, and family services. Taking it a step further, we have also become a lot better at caring for our less tangible needs. The boom in psychology, psychiatry, and self-help industries is an example of this.

The fact that many of us want so badly to spread the wealth and meet basic needs everywhere is proof that self-actualization is possible. That desire is among the earmarks of an actualized person. Actualization provides a whole new human quest for meaning. Whereas before it was enough to work hard, get paid, establish a family, and have a little free time to enjoy, now that is not sufficient. We keep trying to solve the question of meaning and purpose with answers from levels we have already mastered. In other words, we can't earn enough money and buy enough shiny cars, houses, or vacations to make ourselves believe we have lived a meaningful life. We can't eat enough food, either—although god knows we try. When you see nations whose people have to work extremely hard not to get fat, you know that their basic needs have been met, and then some.

We are all called upon to lead with our lives right now.

It is time to step forward and Weird People are singularly equipped to do this because we already have so little interest in following the herd. We have not fit in comfortably heretofore and this means that we are willing to leave the common answers behind in favor of following our hearts. This time is ripe in every way for us to share the gifts of our passion and insight and imagination with the world.

We are rich; we could have free time if we would choose to organize our lives differently; and we have access to all the help and teaching we need to be healthy in body and mind. We have seen an explosion in spirituality and mindfulness practices that are designed to help us live with inner peace. We have no excuse not to move into the highest level of self-actualization.

The trouble is, as a whole, we are not doing it.

We keep building bigger houses and filling them with more expensive things. We live in fancy subdivisions with tidy lawns, but we don't know our neighbors. We have high speed Internet and devices that connect us to an entire universe of information and entertainment, but we feel more isolated than ever before. Instead of using the power tools of our age to streamline our lives, create beautiful things, and solve the remaining problems in the world, we obsess over pictures of some celebrity's ass or get depressed by consuming a constant stream of bad news from around the planet. We worship movie stars and sports heroes rather than play on the stage of our own lives. Then we drive our nice car to a therapist's office, get a prescription for antidepressants, and go to yoga class wearing seventy-dollar stretch pants in hopes of feeling better.

This has to stop.

We cannot leave the business of creating a new world to the anointed few and hope they get it right while we let the clock run out on our lives in a state of comfortable numbness. That is an abdication of our birthright. It denies our own reason for being here at such a remarkable time. We don't need to renounce all of our comforts. We worked hard to get them. But our age cries out to us, pleading, "Wake up! Pay attention. Do something with me." This is an era of unprecedented individual power and freedom—if we will take personal responsibility for our lives and shape them according to our own design.

This means getting ruthless about cutting out what's not real. When I say ruthless, I don't mean cruel or reckless or harsh. I mean uncompromising. I mean unflinchingly honest about what we really want, about what we are afraid of, and about what we are willing to do about it.

There is good news. This is already happening everywhere—not just in the arts. Weird people are coming out and changing business, science, and even government. At the same time, as the world is being rocked by growing terrorist threats and other crises, people are standing up and starting to make change in their own backyards. There is a new breed of entrepreneurs who are building companies that will solve our energy problems and other major issues— probably during our lifetimes. Scientists and engineers are obsessed with breaking through into discoveries that have the potential to tip the scales. Social and political heretics are making waves in places that have always been controlled by dictators. The benevolent virus of human freedom is spreading.

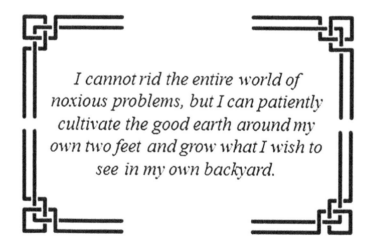

I cannot rid the entire world of noxious problems, but I can patiently cultivate the good earth around my own two feet and grow what I wish to see in my own backyard.

On June 26, 2015, the US Supreme Court overturned the ban on gay marriage. As of right now, it is legal for same-sex couples to marry in every one of the United States. If that's not a weird turn of events compared to how things were at this writing, I don't know what is. It seemed impossible all the way up to the point at which it wasn't. It became possible because people began to stand up and make their voices heard—even though the opposition to this quite reasonable civil liberty appeared to have the upper hand at every level of government.

It is happening.

This is not a time for martyrs. The era of suffering saviors is over. We are not throwing our lives away like cannon fodder in a hopeless war. Our greatest strength and contribution comes from living in joy. By living our truth beautifully in this world, we take our places as leaders. Now is the time and we are the people who can redefine the words "success" and "normal" and yes… "weird."

What we do and the lives we live make a difference. We matter. Interesting, that phrase "we matter." Take that word: "matter." It is related to material—to what is physical—to what we can see, touch, and measure. As the dictionary says: *Matter is physical substance in general, as distinct from mind and spirit; (in physics) that which occupies space and possesses rest mass, especially as distinct from energy.* Our bodies are made of matter and that is its own evidence that we do, indeed, matter.

The very fact that we are here, as ourselves, means something. Our desires to create and express in this world are important. From where I sit, those pure impulses of desire—the insatiable quest to keep searching, trying, experimenting with things that aren't real for us until we find what is—indicate that, however temporary our physical lives and accomplishments might be, the Big Everything really wants to be here through us, as us. It is specific and personal. To put it poetically, we are the fingertips of "God" touching the earth. Hold up your finger. Really. Look at the whorls of your fingerprint. Now close your eyes. Touch your eyebrow. Touch the ground. Notice how much information you receive through the nerve-rich tip of your finger.

Whatever we might call the Great UnBoxable—God, god, Universe, Fred, Nothing, Everything, All That Is, whatever—the vast, non-rational, super-rational, intelligent system seems to want to materialize in the form of humans. Strange, self-conscious, self-loathing, self-aggrandizing, curious, questing, questioning, tasting, fucking, creating, loving, children-having, suffering, heart-beating, breathing, living creatures that we are, we occupy a place unlike any other. We are unique and that means something. What it means is up to us to define, though. That's part of the deal. We, in all of our ridiculous glory, are up to the business of co-defining what life means.

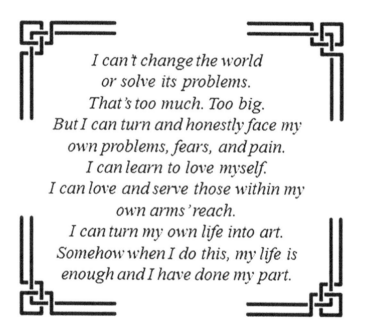

I can't change the world
or solve its problems.
That's too much. Too big.
But I can turn and honestly face my
own problems, fears, and pain.
I can learn to love myself.
I can love and serve those within my
own arms' reach.
I can turn my own life into art.
Somehow when I do this, my life is
enough and I have done my part.

I once took my children on a vacation to the Gulf of Mexico. After a long day of playing in the waves, getting sunburns, and dodging stingrays, they went to bed and I walked back down to the beach. The sun had set and a great full moon was rising above the water. I waded in up to my thighs and had a vision of sorts. In my imagination, I was holding up a glass of wine that represented my life. Under the light of the moon that painted a path of silver across the water, I slowly poured the wine into the ocean. The blood red liquid swirled around my legs and stained the water for a moment and then was gone, washed away in the tide. A silent voice spoke in my mind then. *"You have just changed the chemical composition of the sea forever. It will never be the same. The sea doesn't know it, but it has been changed. This, too, is your life, poured into the great ocean of human experience. They may not know you, but if you pour yourself out completely, you have made a difference in the world. Never doubt this."*

I have doubted it many times since then, of course. The world is large and I am small. My efforts often seem to make little difference. I only know that I am called to fill up the space of my own life with myself, and then pour it all out into the bloodstream of the world. I am called to become. I am called to create. We all are if we will listen.

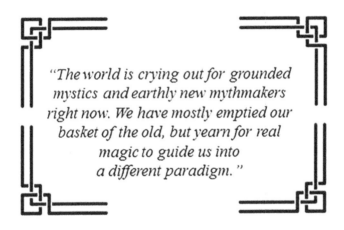

"The world is crying out for grounded mystics and earthly new mythmakers right now. We have mostly emptied our basket of the old, but yearn for real magic to guide us into a different paradigm."

Until now, many of us have felt like aliens on this planet. We get bone weary. We sometimes get discouraged. We just want to go home, wherever that might be. We feel alone and lost at times. We forget that our blood and bones and DNA contain a blueprint for what is coming—for what we are charged to create. The not-normal impulses and urgencies of our nature are the heartbeat of evolution driving us outside the collective comfort zones, forcing us just beyond the horizon—demanding that we keep dreaming and keep taking action toward a work-of-art life and the same kind of world.

We are the line walkers. We spend our lives balancing on the continental divide, one foot on either side of a line that separates the scientific, rational, linear world from the universe of intuition, symbolic information, soul impulses, and the great collective unconscious. Not everyone can handle the tension of living on that knife's edge. Both worlds have powerful magnetic pull on us, and it is easy to lose balance and fall one way or the other—becoming either too rational or too etheric. But this isn't an either-or proposition. Each world informs the other. The literal, concrete world reflects what we have discovered and created thus far. The vast world of the non-rational is rich with imagination and what has not yet been turned into matter. It us up to us—those of us who can bear the constant tension of walking a life-long balance beam—to use the tools and information from both worlds, interlacing them into something beautiful and real.

Joseph Campbell taught us that humans have a persistent zeal to tell stories. We can't seem to help it. He showed us how long, recurring strands connect the religions and myths and legends and cosmologies to each other in the web of our collective consciousness. Over and over again, characters and themes emerge from the soup to illustrate important aspects in the progressive dance of reality and our place in it. Figures like Jesus Christ, Mithra, Dionysus, Lilith, Krishna—all the god-women, god-men, gods, goddesses, angels and demons, heroes and heroines, avatars and super-villains—appear and disappear in recurring cycles of myths that we tell ourselves. Campbell felt that we moderns are crossing a bridge between eras. We have jettisoned many of those old myths, but we have not lost our need for stories and pictures and music and poetry to hold the fabric of our psyches together. We need fresh myths, legends, and heroes to take the place of those we have toppled. That is where we come in. We are weavers. We are sensitive to the electric strands of consciousness that we can't explain, but we can feel them pulsing in us—transmitting crucial information that will help humanity navigate its way into a new era. Weird People—this is who we are and this is our responsibility.

I was watching the TV show *Penny Dreadful* recently and the wicked witch, Evelyn Poole, uttered a phrase that struck me. "A man's character is always his destiny." I love people whose energy imprint is so strong and vivid that it points the way to a unique destiny. Not everyone has this, except perhaps in latent potential, but those who do stand out. Many people have blurry outlines and destiny for them is interchangeable. But Weird People have this sharp-cut quality and must go on epic inner journeys to discover the patterns in the great mosaic of themselves, and then embrace their destiny. This can be a confusing process because it doesn't look like what passes for success or "right path" in other people's lives.

The Hero or Heroine of this type can't use what works for others as reference points to guide them but must endure periods of exploring off the map and feeling lost. Along the way, if they hang on, they learn a radical trust in themselves and the inner compass that becomes their most important instrument to lead them home. And home, in this case, is the great comfort of living deeply real lives that match who they really are.

My own definition of being alive—really alive—has evolved into a dynamic, primitive-but-sophisticated, intuitive jungle dance with the Universe; as dangerous and exciting as it is nourishing and safe. It is a way of being that eats those labels and digests them, swallowing every idea about life and turning them into muscle and blood, nerve and sinew. Until they are no longer distinguishable as concepts, but are absorbed into this magnificent form of a creature that is proud and glad to be here.

So take your books and seminars and retreats and sessions and devour them. Don't leave a scrap lying around uneaten. Pick the bones and crack them open and suck out the marrow. Spit out what doesn't taste good or what you can't swallow. Trust yourself to know what's good for you and what you need for your own adventure.

No idea or book or teacher you assimilate in this passionate way will look the same. They won't be on any kind of pedestal. They will all be invisible but only because they have become part of who you are—a powerful, joyful, fierce artist of life.

Imagine Michelangelo, consumed by his magnificent obsession, standing in the rain with a mallet and chisel over that rough block of marble. He knows that David is waiting to be revealed from the formless mass. He can feel it and, hungry and tired, he raises his hammer again. *Chink... chink... chink.* Sculptors who came before him had rejected this stone because of its flaws and cracks. Michelangelo knows better, though. He knows that it is up to him to liberate the potential he sees in his mind's eye. No one else will do it. No one else can. It is his masterpiece to complete and he won't stop until he has helped the world witness what he has created because he could see through different eyes.

It is exactly the same with us. Whatever our art, we must allow it to consume us. We must give ourselves fully to it and hold our vision as sacred and important. This is when we become leaders. This is when we become examples of what is possible. This is how we fulfill our destiny.

In his book *Factotum*, Charles Bukowski wrote these words that struck a match and lit a torch that still lights the way for all of us soul adventurers, freedom fighters, peace mongers, lovers of life ... for all of us Weird People everywhere:

"If you're going to try, go all the way. Otherwise, don't even start. This could mean losing girlfriends, wives, relatives, and maybe even your mind. It could mean not eating for three or four days. It could mean freezing on a park bench. It could mean jail. It could mean

derision. It could mean mockery—isolation. Isolation is the gift. All the others are a test of your endurance, of how much you really want to do it. And, you'll do it, despite rejection and the worst odds. And it will be better than anything else you can imagine. If you're going to try, go all the way. There is no other feeling like that. You will be alone with the gods, and the nights will flame with fire. You will ride life straight to perfect laughter. It's the only good fight there is."

AFTERWORD

Your Life Is Your Art

The whole point of this book comes down to this.
Your life is your art.

I mentioned my friend and fellow renaissance human, Andréa Balt, earlier. She uses that phrase a lot. I don't just like it. It's true.

What's true is that we are all artists. Each of us paints on the canvas of our lives. Every moment is a new brush stroke. Most of us are unconscious of that, except maybe in brief flashes of awareness.

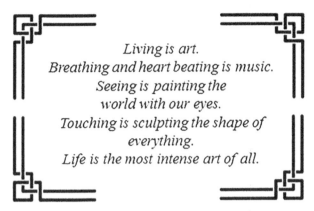

Living is art.
Breathing and heart beating is music.
Seeing is painting the
world with our eyes.
Touching is sculpting the shape of
everything.
Life is the most intense art of all.

Being unconscious about it leads to a life created unconsciously—and that means feeling like a victim of circumstances. It is so easy to forget that every single choice I make is another brush stroke. All of them are.

This whole thing is about consciously lifting the brush, stepping up in front of the canvas of our lives, and choosing what shapes and colors will appear.

In my deepest heart, I carry the cries of Blessed Weird people from everywhere and every-when. Your cries are echoes of my own. Your struggles and passions are mine, too.

Let's get so real and clear and strong that we won't wait around for anyone's permission to show up as ourselves.

Let's flood the world with passion and beauty.

Let's rise up and paint the world with the colors of our hearts—with our books and paintings and music and groovy businesses and inventions and children and ideas … and with just everything that's possible when people do their truest things here.

Your life is your art. Your life is your manifesto. All true art is a manifesto of its creator, and every true manifesto is art.

Hayao Miyazaki said, *"Whenever someone creates something with all of their heart, then that creation is given a soul."* I can ask nothing more for this book or my life—that it be given a soul. The truth is, my job with this book has nearly ended. I must now turn this work of my heart over to the world—to you. As with any art, the creator must collaborate with the lovers of art if it has a chance of becoming what it can be. Should this book touch your heart, the act of reading it, talking about it, and living out what feels alive in it for yourself is what fills in the remaining empty places of this mosaic. In other words, you are my fellow creator.

This book is now ended, but my life has not yet, so I step forward from here to create the rest of it with all of my heart. Thank you for being here.

Your fellow traveler, Jacob Nordby

Thank Yous, Fuck Yous, Chapter Notes, and Whathaveyous

Mostly I hate reading acknowledgment sections, so I don't do it. Neither do you. That's why I get to say whatever I want right now with almost no risk of offending anyone. The book's over. Anyway, most acknowledgement pages are filled with thanking people who …

1). None of us knows, but the author couldn't have done it without or at least wants them to believe that so they will keep doing nice things or having sex with them or whatever,

2). All of us know and the author is dropping names, or (in the case of a really shitty book),

3). Should have drowned the author before he/she started writing and saved the world from more shitty books.

I will certainly thank people who belong in each category. My mother thinks that I should not have listed number three or at least not suggested that this is possibly a shitty book. Thank you, Mom! That, along with giving birth to me and encouraging all sorts of magic throughout my life, just earned you the very first thank you. You are amazing and wise and batshit crazy (no, yes you are—it's my book and I get to say that) and I love you very much.

Also, I couldn't bring myself to do a proper bibliography. I'll try to mention some sources or important books later in this clean up round. You aren't reading this, so it doesn't matter, but perhaps this section will save my ass from a lawsuit.

Randy Davila is a great friend, mentor, and also a publisher. He not only encouraged me to write this book, but also read the first terrible draft and gave me extremely helpful critique (which I both appreciated and hated at the time). I work for two of his companies and our connection has become something for which I am grateful every day. If he reads the final version of this book, I hope to still have a job because I like working with him very much. I'm pretty much counting on the probability that he (like you) will never read this section.

Craig Hart served as my sounding board and long-suffering developmental editor. Based upon how well I did or did not take advice from him, he may or may not appreciate being mentioned here. I have known Craig since we were both a lot younger. He's one of my best friends and that friendship has managed to survive my apostasy, a divorce from his sister, and many occasions of me tilting at windmills—and asking him to go along for the ride even though he knew better. He's a fine writer and a finer human. (If you were a girl, I'd marry you, Craig. Swear to god I would.) Ask Google about "Craig Alan Hart" and also find him on Amazon.

Beth Lynne, Ed.D. is my editor. She is also known as BZ Hercules. I haven't allowed her to read this section either. I am grateful for both her technical abilities and the incisive questions that she asked during the process of cleaning up this book. Turns out, she has a keen sense of humor and I wish that I could have included all of her editing notes, but then you would wonder why you were reading my book and not hers.

Lisa Braun Dubbels is a quiet PR professional who represents an impressive list of who's-who types. She is also quirkily selective and makes up her own rules about who gets any of her time. For that reason, I am grateful for her help and advice—and for a behind-the-scenes friendship that brings me a lot of joy and laughter.

I have attempted to properly thank, quote, and credit people throughout the text whose words and lives have influenced me. Here is a handful of additional notes that I need to include before I get back to thank yous:

The Ernest Hemingway excerpt in Chapter Four was borrowed from his book, *A Farewell to Arms*, published by Charles Scribner's Sons, 1957.

In Chapter Five I quoted words from the *Tao Te Ching*. These are from a translation by Stephen Mitchell, published by Harper Perennial.

In Chapter Seven, I wrote about Banksy and used as my source an article by Kurt Kohlstedt, *The Banksy Paradox: 7 Sides to the World's Most Infamous Street Artist,* which can be found on Weburbanist. com.

Chapters Seven and Eight contained information about Leonardo da Vinci and the troubadours for which I must credit *The Templar Revelation* by Lynn Picknett and Clive Prince; published by Touchstone.

Robert Anton Wilson's book *Prometheus Rising* found me, as many others have done, at a time during which I was struggling with how to find my own freedom—mental, spiritual, and physical. It is (and he was) about as weird as they get, and I highly recommend it for those who love to question everything.

I have quoted and sourced Abraham Maslow extensively throughout this book. His *The Farther Reaches of Human Nature* is a dense-but-fascinating excursion into the mind of this human potentialist. He wrote plenty of other stuff, but I haven't read most of it yet. You should, though, and then come tell me about it (but only if you can do it in an interesting way). And now back to a few final thank yous.

My family is an intense tribe. We fight, laugh, adventure, talk endlessly, and weep together—often all at the same time. There's no way I can thank them enough for how they have provided me with mirrors, grist for the mill, and fuel for the journey. My youngest brother, Andrew, has been my particular companion during this project and our conversations have ranged over a vast spectrum—

each time forcing me to expand my own vision. Plus, he's a pirate and helps me keep it real. Thanks, bro.

Barb Black is my friend and confidant and as weird as they come in the best possible way. She painted the original Blessed Are the Weird poster art and inspires me with all sorts of profane wisdom and laughter. Please finish your book, Barb.

Melinda is among my weirdest, wisest of friends. Also, she's an expert astrologer, witchy woman, and a writer. Thanks for everything, M. You know what I mean.

There are several trusted people in my circle who served as early readers. Thank you. I mostly didn't take your advice, but please don't interpret this as an insult. The fact that you were willing to take a look at the hot mess at all gave me courage to keep chiseling away at this thing.

And thank you to all Blessed Weirdians everywhere… past, present, and future… without you, I would not have had any idea that there was a book to be written. You picked up those first early words and spread them. Since that time, you have supported, shared stuff, argued with, and inspired me. I could not have kept going (in fact, I tried any number of times to stop, but you wouldn't stop, so I couldn't) without you—and I still can't, so let's keep doing this together, shall we?

I don't have a long list of fuck yous. Those seem to happen in real time and fade quickly. I tend not to hold grudges.

However, there are a few perennial offenders:

People who want to nitpick semantics or analyze concepts to death and miss the whole point.

Anyone who tries to limit human freedom, passion, and creativity in others. I think that we all do a more-than-adequate job of that for ourselves, so fuck off.

People who bully others with their words, bodies, ideas, or positions. Fuck you. Really a lot. (Yes, yes… I know. Everyone is doing their best and <insert other lofty concept here>. But still, stop it and go fuck yourself until you can learn to behave better.)

Since none of these recidivists could possibly still be reading (and they wouldn't read a book like this anyway), I will end now with a last, long *thank you*! Thank you for joining me on this grand adventure. Perhaps our paths will cross somewhere in the wilderness. In the meantime, fair winds in your sails and sun on your face.

Connect with Jacob and the Weirdians

You may find Jacob Nordby on his website
and social media sites

www.JacobNordby.com
facebook.com/author.jacobnordby

Be sure to sign up for email updates,
and learn about his other books and writings!

Visit www.BlessedAreTheWeird.com
to find out what's up in the tribe of Weirdians

Made in the USA
Las Vegas, NV
08 January 2022

40851929R00111